SEVEN SHORT PLAYS
BY ANTON CHEKHOV

The Bear, A Reluctant Tragic Hero, Swan Song, The Proposal, The Dangers of Tobacco, The Festivities, The Wedding Reception

A NEW TRANSLATION
BY PAUL SCHMIDT

★

★

DRAMATISTS
PLAY SERVICE
INC.

TABLE OF CONTENTS

THE BEAR

A COMIC SKETCH IN ONE ACT

1888

CHARACTERS

YELÉNA IVÁNOVNA POPÓVA — a widow with dimples and
a large estate

GRIGÓRY STEPÁNOVICH SMÍRNOFF — landowner,
in his thirties

LUKÁ — an elderly servant

The action takes place in Popóva's living room.

THE BEAR

Popóva's living room. Popóva, dressed completely in black, sits staring at a photograph. Luká, her old servant, tries to talk sense to her.

LUKÁ.   It's just not right, missus. You're letting yourself fall to pieces. Cook and the maid have gone berry picking, every living thing is out enjoying the sunshine, even your cat, now, he's out there trying to catch himself a bird, and here you sit, shut up in the house all day long, like some kind of nun. That's no fun. You listen to what I'm saying, now! It's been a whole year since you left the house!

POPÓVA.   I shall never leave this house. Why should I? My life is over. He's dead and buried, and so am I, buried here within these four walls. We're both dead.

LUKÁ.   I never heard the like! Your husband's dead. Well, God rest him, he's not coming back. You mourned him good and proper; now it's time to move on. You can't sit here wearing black and crying for the rest of your life. I lost my old woman, too, a while back, I cried for a month, and that was that. No need to sit around for years singing hymns; she wasn't worth it. *(Sighs.)* You haven't seen your neighbors in months, you don't go out, and you tell us not to let anybody in. We're all living like spiders in the dark here, if you'll excuse the expression. My livery jacket's got moth holes. Fine, if there was nobody around worth seeing, but the whole county's crawling with eligible young men. There's a regiment in the next town, all those good-looking officers, melt in your mouth, most of them, and they have a dance every Friday night, and the band gives a concert every afternoon. Oh, missus, take a look at yourself — you're still a juicy young thing, you're still beautiful, you can go out and enjoy life. But a beautiful

7

face won't last forever, you know. You wait — ten years from now you're going to want to go swanning after those officers, and it'll be too late.

POPÓVA. *(Firmly.)* I must ask you never to talk to me like this again! When my husband died, life lost all meaning for me. You know that. I may look like I'm alive, but I'm not. I swore I'd wear black and shut myself up here until the day I die, didn't I? And I will. He'll see how much I loved him ... Oh, I know he treated me badly — I don't have to tell you about it. He was mean and ... and even unfaithful. But I intend to be faithful to the grave and show him what *real* love means.

LUKÁ. That's just a lot of talk. You'd do better to go out and take a walk, or have me hitch up Toby and go visit the neighbors.

POPÓVA. Oh! *(Bursts into hysterical tears.)*

LUKÁ. Missus! What is it? For God's sake, what's the matter?

POPÓVA. Toby! He used to love Toby so! He'd ride all over the neighborhood on him. What a horseman! Remember how grand he looked in the saddle? Oh, Toby, Toby! Go tell them he gets extra oats today.

LUKÁ. *(Sighs.)* Don't worry, I will. *(The doorbell rings. And keeps ringing.)*

POPÓVA. *(Exasperated.)* Now who's that? Go tell whoever it is I am not at home! To anyone!

LUKÁ. Whatever you say, missus. *(Goes out.)*

POPÓVA. *(To the photograph.)* You see what real love means, Nicky? My love will last as long as I do, right to my last heartbeat. *(Laughs, almost crying.)* And I hope you're ashamed of yourself! You see what a good girl I am, what a faithful wife? I locked myself up here and will be faithful to you till the day I die, while you ... I hope you're ashamed, you little pig. You were mean to me, you cheated on me, you left me alone for weeks at a time — *(Enter Luká; he's upset.)*

LUKÁ. Missus, there's someone wants to see you. Says it can't wait.

POPÓVA. Didn't you tell him that my husband is dead and that I see no one?

LUKÁ. I did, but he doesn't want to listen, says it's very important.

POPÓVA. And I said I see no one!

LUKÁ. That's what I told him, but he's ... he's kind of a wild

8

man — he started shouting and pushed his way into the house. He's in the dining room right now.

POPÓVA.   All right, all right, tell him all right. Really! The nerve of some people! *(Luká goes out.)* Why must people be so difficult? Why can't they just leave me alone? *(Sighs.)* Oh, I may have to go join a nunnery after all. *(Thinks.)* I wonder what kind of nun I'd make ... *(Enter Smírnoff; trailed by Luká.)*

SMÍRNOFF.   *(To Luká.)* You dingbat, stop trying to talk me out of here! Idiot! *(Sees Popóva; suddenly very dignified.)* Ah, madam. Let me introduce myself: Grigóry Stepánovich Smírnoff, Field Artillery, retired. I own a place over in the next county. Sorry to disturb you, but this is important —

POPÓVA.   *(Doesn't offer him her hand.)* What can I do for you?

SMÍRNOFF.   I had the pleasure of knowing your late husband, and as it happens, he left me two IOUs — the total comes to twelve hundred rubles. Now, I have a mortgage payment due tomorrow, so I have to ask you, madam, to pay up. And I'm afraid I need the money today.

POPÓVA.   Twelve hundred? What did my husband owe you the money for?

SMÍRNOFF.   I sold him a couple of loads of oats.

POPÓVA.   *(With a sigh, to Luká.)* Now don't forget what I told you, Luká. You make sure Toby gets his extra oats. *(Luká goes out. To Smírnoff.)* If my husband owed you the money, then of course I'll pay it, but you'll have to excuse me — I don't have any cash on me today. My manager will be back from town the day after tomorrow, and he'll see that you get paid. But today, I'm afraid, I cannot help you. It's exactly seven months today that my husband died, and I'm in a sad mood. I'm in no condition to talk about money.

SMÍRNOFF.   *(Annoyed.)* And I'm in a sad mood too, because if I don't meet my mortgage payment tomorrow, they'll foreclose on my property! I'll lose my shirt!

POPÓVA.   You'll have your money the day after tomorrow.

SMÍRNOFF.   I need the money today, not the day after tomorrow.

POPÓVA.   Excuse me; I've already said I cannot pay you today.

SMÍRNOFF.   And I've already said I can't wait till the day after tomorrow.

9

POPÓVA.   What can I do? I don't *have* the money!

SMÍRNOFF.   That means you won't pay me?

POPÓVA.   It means I *can't* pay you!

SMÍRNOFF.   I see. Is that your final word?

POPÓVA.   That is my final word.

SMÍRNOFF.   You've made up your mind?

POPÓVA.   I've made up my mind.

SMÍRNOFF.   Thank you very much. I won't forget this. *(Shrugs.)* Am I supposed to take all this lying down? On my way here, I met my accountant. "Why are you always so down in the dumps?" he asks me. Well, excuse me, he should know! I'm desperate for money! I got up at dawn yesterday and rode around to everyone I know who owes me money, and not a one of them came across! I ran in more circles than a hunting dog, spent the night in some godforsaken fleabag hotel, and finally I get here, fifty miles from home, expect to get paid, and what do I get? "A sad mood"! What kind of mood do you think that puts *me* in?

POPÓVA.   I think I made myself perfectly clear: I'll pay you as soon as my manager gets back from town.

SMÍRNOFF.   I came to see you, not your manager! What the hell — excuse my language — do I want with your manager?

POPÓVA.   My dear sir, I will not have such language in my house, nor will I tolerate that tone of voice! I refuse to listen to any more of this! *(Storms out.)*

SMÍRNOFF.   I don't believe this! "It's seven months today my husband died, and I'm in a sad mood ..." What's that got to do with me? I have to make a mortgage payment! Fine, your husband's dead, your manager's gone to town, you're in a mood or whatever — what do you expect me to do? Flap my wings and fly away from my creditors? Run around banging my head into a brick wall? I go see Grúzdeff, he's not home. I go see Yarosévich, he hides. I go see Kurítsyn, we get into a fight; I damn near threw him out his own window. I go see Mazútov, he's sick. And now this one has "a sad mood." Not a one of them paid me! What a bunch of deadbeats! And it's all because I'm such a soft touch, I'm a sucker for a hard-luck story! I'm too nice for my own good! Well, it's time to get a little tough. Nobody's going to fool around with me like this, goddamn it! I'm not moving; I'm staying put until she pays up! Oh, boy, am I mad! Look at me — I'm quivering mad! Mad through and through, goddamn it! Mad enough to get nasty! *(Shouts.)* Hey, you! *(Enter Luká.)*

LUKÁ. What do you want?

SMÍRNOFF. A glass of water. Or better yet, a beer. *(Luká goes out.)* What kind of logic is that? Here's a man so desperate for money he's ready to hang himself, and she can't pay him because — excuse me very much — she's "in no condition to talk about money." Talk about petticoat logic! This is why I don't like women and hate talking to them. I'd rather light a campfire on a powder keg than talk to a woman. Makes my skin crawl, they make me so mad! All I have to do is see one of those romantic creatures coming, my leg muscles start cramping up. I want to start shouting for help. *(Enter Luká.)*

LUKÁ. *(Brings Smírnoff a glass of water.)* The missus is sick; she says she can't see anybody!

SMÍRNOFF. Get out of here! *(Luká goes out.)* She's sick and she can't see anybody! That's fine; she doesn't have to see me. I'll just stay right here until I get my money, that's all. She stays sick for a week, I stay here for a week. She's sick for a year, I stay here for a year. I want my money, lady! Your black dress and your dimples don't impress me. I've seen plenty of dimples before! *(Goes to the window and shouts.)* Hey, Semyón, unhitch the horses! We're not leaving just yet! I'm staying right here! Tell them in the stable to give my horses some oats! And watch it, you nitwit — you've got the trace horse tangled again! You just wait till I get ... oh, forget it. *(Moves away from the window.)* Jesus, what a mess. Hottest day of the year, nobody wants to pay me, couldn't sleep the whole night, and now I've got to deal with some wacky widow and her moods. It's enough to give a man a headache. I need a drink, that's what I need. *(Yells.)* Hey, you! *(Enter Luká.)*

LUKÁ. What do you want?

SMÍRNOFF. A shot of vodka! *(Luká goes out; Smírnoff falls into a chair and looks himself over.)* Oof, I'm a mess. Dirt, mud on my boots, I need a shave, my hair needs combing, straw sticking out of my pockets. The lady must have thought I was out to rob her. *(Yawns.)*

Not too polite, I guess, showing up like this, but what the hell ...
I'm not a guest, I'm a bill collector; nobody says I have to dress
right ... *(Enter Luká; he gives Smírnoff a glass of vodka.)*
LUKÁ.   You take too many liberties, you know that...?
SMÍRNOFF.   *(Angry.)* What?
LUKÁ.   Oh, nothing. I just ... Nothing.
SMÍRNOFF.   Who do you think you're talking to? Just shut up,
will you?
LUKÁ.   *(Aside, as he goes out.)* How're we going to get rid of him...?
SMÍRNOFF.   Oh, I'm mad! I am so mad! Mad enough to blow
up the world! Mad enough to get nasty! *(Shouts.)* Hey, you! *(Enter
Popóva.)*
POPÓVA.   *(Not looking at him.)* My dear sir, I have lived so long in
retirement I have grown unused to the human voice. I cannot
stand shouting. I must earnestly beg you to respect my solitude.
SMÍRNOFF.   Pay me my money and I'll go.
POPÓVA.   I have told you in no uncertain terms that I have no
money here at the moment and you will have to wait until the day
after tomorrow.
SMÍRNOFF.   And I also told you in no uncertain terms that
I need the money today, not the day after tomorrow. If you
don't pay me today, I might as well hang myself by the day after
tomorrow.
POPÓVA.   But what can I do, since I don't have the money?
SMÍRNOFF.   You mean you're not going to pay me? Is that what
you mean?
POPÓVA.   I can't!
SMÍRNOFF.   In that case, I stay right here until I get it. *(Sits
down.)* You're going to pay me the day after tomorrow? Fine. I'll
be sitting right here! *(Jumps up.)* Look, don't you believe I have a
mortgage payment due tomorrow? You think I'm joking?
POPÓVA.   I asked you not to shout! You're not in a stable.
SMÍRNOFF.   I didn't ask you about a stable! What I asked you
was, "Don't you believe I have a mortgage payment due tomorrow?"
POPÓVA.   You haven't the faintest idea of how to behave in a
lady's presence.
SMÍRNOFF.   I do so know how to behave in a lady's presence!

POPÓVA.   No, you do not! You are ill-mannered and vulgar! No gentleman would speak like this in front of a lady!

SMÍRNOFF.   Oh, well, excuse me! Just how would he speak in front of a lady? In French? *(With a nasty lisp.)* *Madame, je vous prie* ... How charmed I am to know that you reject to pay me my money! Ah, *pardon*, I seem to be upsetting you! Lovely weather we're having! And my, my, don't you look lovely in black! *(Makes a fake bow.)*

POPÓVA.   You're being very stupid and not funny.

SMÍRNOFF.   *(Mocking.)* Stupid and not funny! I don't know how to behave in a lady's presence! Woman, I have seen more ladies in my time than you have seen sparrows in yours! I have fought three duels because of ladies, I have walked out on twelve ladies, and nine ladies have walked out on me! So there! Oh, I used to be an idiot, got crushes on them, sweet-talked, cast my pearls before — Well ... Bow, click my heels, fall in love, suffer, sigh in the moonlight, freeze up, melt into puddles — I did it all. I could rattle on for hours about women's rights: I spent half my life hanging around women, but not anymore! No, thank you very much! No more wool over my eyes! I've had it! Dark eyes, red lips, dimples in the cheeks, moonlight, sighs of passion — no, sir, I wouldn't give you two cents for any of it now. Present company excepted, of course, but all women are pretentious, affected, gossipy, hateful, liars to the marrow of their bones, vain, petty, merciless, they can't think straight, and as for this part here *(Slaps his forehead.)* ... well — excuse my frankness — a sparrow has ten times more brains than any philosopher in skirts. Take a good look at any one of these romantic creatures: petticoats and hot air, divine transports, the whole works; then take a look at her soul. Pure crocodile. *(Grabs the back of a chair; the chair cracks and breaks.)* And the worst part is, this crocodile thinks she has a monopoly on the tender emotion of love! Goddamn it, has any woman ever known how to love anything except her lapdog? She's in love, all she can do is snivel and whine. A man in love, now, he suffers and sacrifices, but a woman, her love shows up how? She swishes her skirt and gets a firm grip on your nose. You're a woman, unfortunately, but at least you know what I mean, what woman's nature is like. Tell me honestly: Have you ever seen a woman who was faithful and true? No, you haven't! The only honest and faithful women are old or ugly.

POPÓVA. Excuse me, but would you mind telling me just who you think *is* faithful and true? Men?

SMÍRNOFF. Well, of course, men.

POPÓVA. Men! *(A mean laugh.)* Men are faithful and true in love! Well, spread the good news! *(Hotly.)* How dare you say that? Men faithful and true? Let me tell you a thing or two! Of all the men I know or have ever known, my dear departed husband was the best. I loved him passionately, with all my heart and soul, the way only a young and sensitive girl can love; I gave him my youth, my happiness, my life, my money; I lived and breathed for him, I worshiped him, he was my idol, and ... and what do you think he did? This best of all possible men betrayed me in the worst possible way: He cheated on me every chance he got. After he died I found boxes and boxes of love letters in his desk! And when he was alive he'd leave me alone for weeks on end. And he flirted with other women right in front of me, he deceived me, he spent all my money, he laughed at me when I objected. And despite everything, I loved him, and I will be faithful to his memory. Even though he's dead, I am faithful and unshakable. I have buried myself within these four walls, where I shall mourn him forever. I shall wear black until the day I die.

SMÍRNOFF. *(A sneering laugh.)* Black? Don't make me laugh! How dumb do you think I am? I know exactly why you go around in that Mardi Gras outfit and why you've buried yourself within these walls! Of course! It's all so romantic, so mysterious! You're waiting for some shavetail army lieutenant to come riding by, or some sentimental schoolboy with a bad complexion, and he'll look up at your window and think: Ah! There dwells the mysterious Tamara, who loved her husband so much she buried herself within four walls ... I know all about your little games.

POPÓVA. *(Flares up.)* What? How dare you even suggest anything of the kind!

SMÍRNOFF. You buried yourself alive, but you didn't forget to powder your nose!

POPÓVA.   How dare you!! How dare you speak to me like this!

SMÍRNOFF.   Don't yell at me — I'm not your manager. But I'm a man, not a woman, and I'm used to calling a spade a spade. And please stop shouting.

POPÓVA.   I'm not shouting — you are! Will you please go away and leave me alone!

SMÍRNOFF.   Pay me my money and I'll go!

POPÓVA.   I will not give you any money!

SMÍRNOFF.   You will too!

POPÓVA.   I will not! You won't get one red cent from me! Now please go away!

SMÍRNOFF.   I do not have the pleasure of being either your husband or your fiance, so please stop making scenes for my benefit. *(Sits down.)* I hate that.

POPÓVA.   *(Snorting with anger.)* You dare sit down?

SMÍRNOFF.   Exactly.

POPÓVA.   Will you please go!

SMÍRNOFF.   Just give me my money! *(Aside.)* Oh, am I mad! Am I *mad!*

POPÓVA.   Of all the nerve! I want nothing more to do with you! Please leave! *(Pause.)* You're still here? You haven't left?

SMÍRNOFF.   No.

POPÓVA.   No?

SMÍRNOFF.   No.

POPÓVA.   All right! *(Rings. Enter Luká.)* Luká, will you please show this gentleman out?

LUKÁ.   *(Goes over to Smírnoff.)* Please leave, sir. The lady asked you to. She doesn't want you here.

SMÍRNOFF.   *(Leaps to his feet.)* And you shut up! Who do you think you're talking to? I'll make a tossed salad out of you!

LUKÁ.   *(Clutches his heart.)* Oh, my God! Oh, mother of God! *(Falls into an armchair.)* I'm dying! I'm dying! I can't breathe!

POPÓVA.   Dásha! Where's Dásha? *(Screams.)* Dásha! Pelégea! Dásha! *(Rings frantically.)*

LUKÁ.   They all went off berry picking. There's nobody else in the house! Oh, I'm dying! Water!

POPÓVA.   Will you get out of here?

SMÍRNOFF.   Can't you be a little more polite?

POPÓVA.   *(Makes a fist and stamps her foot.)* You peasant! You bear! You vulgar bear! Monster! You ... *radical!*

SMÍRNOFF.   What? What did you call me?

POPÓVA.   I said you were a bear!

SMÍRNOFF.   *(Moves toward her.)* And just who said you could insult me like that?

POPÓVA.   You're right, I am insulting you! What about it? You think I'm afraid of you?

SMÍRNOFF.   You think, just because you're some kind of romantic heroine, that gives you the right to insult me with impunity? Is that it? Oh, no! This is a matter for the field of honor!

LUKÁ.   Oh, my God! Oh, my God! Water!

SMÍRNOFF.   Time to choose weapons!

POPÓVA.   And just because you've got big fists and a bull neck, you think I'm afraid of you? You ... you bear!

SMÍRNOFF.   To the field of honor! Nobody insults me like that, not even a woman!

POPÓVA.   *(Trying to shout him down.)* Bear! Bear! Bear!

SMÍRNOFF.   It's about time we got rid of old prejudices about only men needing to defend themselves on the field of honor! If it's equality you want, then it's equality you get! I challenge you to a duel!

POPÓVA.   You want to fight a duel! Good! Let's fight!

SMÍRNOFF.   Right this minute!

POPÓVA.   Right this minute! My husband had a set of pistols; wait here, I'll go get them. *(Starts out and immediately returns.)* Goddamn you! You have no idea what a pleasure it will be for me to put a bullet through your thick head! *(Goes out.)*

SMÍRNOFF.   I'll shoot her like a sitting duck! I'm not a schoolboy anymore, I'm no sentimental puppy — I don't care if she *is* the weaker sex!

LUKÁ.   Oh, please, sir! *(Falls to his knees.)* Please don't do this, please just leave, please. I'm an old man, my heart won't stand all the excitement! Please don't shoot her!

SMÍRNOFF.   *(Pays no attention to him.)* I'll shoot her — that's real equality; that'll emancipate her! Equality of the sexes at last! But what a woman! *(Imitates her.)* "Goddamn you! You have no idea

what a pleasure it will be to put a bullet through your thick head!"
Yes, what a woman! She got all flushed; her eyes were flashing fire;
she accepted my challenge without even thinking! By God, that's
the first time this has ever happened to me!

LUKÁ.   Oh, please, sir, please go! Just go away!

SMÍRNOFF.   Now, that's a woman I understand! That's a real
woman! She's not one of your sissies, nothing wishy-washy about
her; she's all flint and firepower! I'm almost sorry to have to
kill her!

LUKÁ.   *(Cries.) Please, sir, please,* just go! Please!

SMÍRNOFF.   I definitely like this woman! Definitely! So she has
dimples — I still like her. I'm almost ready to tell her to forget
about the money. And I'm not mad anymore ... What an aston-
ishing woman! *(Enter Popóva; she carries a pair of dueling pistols.)*

POPÓVA.   Here're the pistols. But before we have our duel, will
you please show me how to use the damn things? I've never even
touched one before.

LUKÁ.   Oh, God have mercy on us all! I'm going to get the gardener and the coachman ... Why did this have to happen to us...?

SMÍRNOFF.   *(Looks over the pistols with a professional eye.)* You
see, there are several different makes of weapon. You've got your
Mortimer, now — that's a special dueling pistol, percussion
action. But what you have here are Smith and Wesson revolvers,
triple action, with an extractor and central sights. Beautiful
pieces! Must have cost at least ninety rubles the pair. Now look,
you hold the pistol like this ... *(Aside.)* What amazing eyes she's
got! What a little spitfire!

POPÓVA.   Like this?

SMÍRNOFF.   That's it, that's the way. Next you cock the piece,
like this ... and you take aim ... Move your head back a little.
Stretch out your arm ... that's the way. Then you press your finger
on this little thing here, and that's all there is to it. Main thing
is, keep your cool and take slow, careful aim. Try not to let your
hand shake.

POPÓVA.   Right ... We shouldn't shoot indoors — let's go outside.

SMÍRNOFF.   All right, let's go outside. Only I warn you, I intend
to shoot into the air.

POPÓVA.   Oh, that's the last straw! Why?

SMÍRNOFF. Because ... because ... It's none of your business why!

POPÓVA. Are you getting scared? Is that it? Aha, that's it! Oh no, you won't get out of this so easily! Come on, we're going outside! I won't rest until I put a bullet through that head of yours — that head I hate so! What's the matter, are you a coward?

SMÍRNOFF. That's it, I'm a coward.

POPÓVA. You're lying! Why don't you want to fight?

SMÍRNOFF. Because ... because ... because I like you.

POPÓVA. *(Sarcastic laugh.)* He likes me! He dares to tell me he likes me! *(Points to the door.)* Just go.

SMÍRNOFF. *(Puts down the pistol in silence, takes his hat, and starts out; at the door, he stops and turns. They look at each other in silence for a moment; then he goes hesitantly toward Popóva.)* Listen ... are you still mad? I was crazy myself until just a minute ago, but you know ... how can I put it? Well, the fact is, I ... you see, the fact is, nothing like this ever happened to me before ... *(Shouts.)* Well, goddamn it, is it my fault I like you? *(Grabs a chair behind his back; the chair cracks and breaks.)* Why do you have such fragile furniture! I like you! You understand? I ... I think I'm in love with you!

POPÓVA. Get away from me! I hate you!

SMÍRNOFF. God, what a woman! I've never seen anything like her in my entire life! I'm done for! I'm caught in her mousetrap!

POPÓVA. Get away from me, or I'll shoot!

SMÍRNOFF. Go ahead, shoot! You don't know how happy that will make me, to die with your beautiful eyes upon me, die from a gun in your silky little hand ... Oh, I'm out of my mind! Look, you'd better think this over fast and decide right away. Once I leave here, we'll never see each other again. Make up your mind. I own a lot of land, I'm from a good family, I've got an income of ten thousand a year ... I can put a bullet through a coin in the air at twenty paces ... I've got the best horses you'll ever see ... Will you marry me?

POPÓVA. *(Angry, she waves the pistol.)* Marry you? I intend to shoot you! On the field of honor!

SMÍRNOFF. I'm out of my mind! I don't understand what's happening ...

POPÓVA. On the field of honor!

SMÍRNOFF.   I'm out of my mind! I'm in love! I'm behaving like an idiot schoolboy! *(Grabs her hand; she shrieks with pain.)* I love you! *(Falls to his knees.)* I love you, the way I've never loved anyone before! I walked out on twelve women, nine walked out on me, but I never loved one of them the way I do you! My mind has turned to jelly, my joints have turned to sugar, I'm on my knees like a dope, and I'm asking for your hand ... Oh, the shame, the shame! I haven't been in love for six years, I swore I never would again, and all of a sudden I'm head over heels! I'm asking you to marry me! Yes or no? Will you? Yes or no? No? Fine! *(Gets up and heads quickly toward the door.)*

POPÓVA.   Wait a minute ...

SMÍRNOFF.   *(Stops.)* Well?

POPÓVA.   Nothing, just go! No, I mean, wait ... No, go away! Go away! I hate you! I mean, no, don't go! Oh, you make me so mad! *(Throws the pistol on the floor.)* My finger's all swollen up from that damn thing! *(Starts tearing her handkerchief.)* Well, what are you waiting for? Just get out of here!

SMÍRNOFF.   All right, then. Good-bye.

POPÓVA.   Yes, yes, just go! *(Screams.)* Where are you going? Wait a minute ... Oh, come on back. Oh, I'm so mad! Stay away from me! Stay away from me!

SMÍRNOFF.   *(Crosses to her.)* You're mad? *I'm* mad! I fell in love like a schoolboy, got down on my knees, I even got goose bumps ... *(Roughly.)* I love you! That's all I needed, to fall in love with you! Tomorrow I've got to pay the mortgage, start cutting hay, and now you — *(Grabs her around the waist.)* I'll never forgive myself for this —

POPÓVA.   Get away from me! Get your hands off me! I ... I hate you! I want to fight the d-d-duel! *(A long kiss. Enter Luká with a shovel, the gardener with a rake, the coachman with a pitchfork, some farmworkers with sticks.)*

LUKÁ.   *(Sees the couple kissing.)* Oh, my God ... *(Pause.)*

POPÓVA.   *(Shyly.)* Luká, go out to the stable and tell them Toby doesn't get extra oats anymore.

CURTAIN.

19

PROPERTY LIST

Glass of water (LUKÁ)
Glass of vodka (LUKÁ)
Dueling pistols (POPÓVA)
Handkerchief (POPÓVA)
Shovel (LUKÁ)
Rake (GARDENER)
Pitchfork (COACHMAN)
Sticks (FARMWORKERS)

SOUND EFFECTS

Doorbell

A RELUCTANT TRAGIC HERO

(A SCENE FROM COUNTRY LIFE)

A COMIC SKETCH IN ONE ACT

1889

CHARACTERS

IVÁN IVÁNOVICH TOLKACHÓV — a family man
ALEXÉY ALEXÉYEVICH MURÁSHKIN — his friend

The action takes place in St. Petersburg,
in Muráshkin's apartment.

A RELUCTANT TRAGIC HERO

A room. Muráshkin alone. Enter Tolkachóv.

MURÁSHKIN.   Iván Ivánich! Good to see you! What brings you here?

TOLKACHÓV.   *(Breathing heavily.)* Favor. Please! You're my friend, you have to ... Favor. I'm in trouble, real trouble; I need your help. Can you lend me a gun? Please! Just till tomorrow. Be a friend. Do me a favor.

MURÁSHKIN.   What do you need a gun for?

TOLKACHÓV.   What do I need a gun for...? Oh, boy. Oh boy oh boy oh boy. Give me a drink. Have to have something to drink. Fast. A glass of water, have to have water ... See, I ... Well, the fact is, I'm going to be spending the night out in the woods alone, way out in the woods, so I ... You know. Just in case anything happens. So can you lend me a gun? Please! Do me a favor!

MURÁSHKIN.   Iván Ivánich, you're not making any sense! What's all this woods business? You sound like Little Red Riding Hood. Are you in trouble? You're involved in something illegal, right? What's happened? What's the matter with you? You look sick.

TOLKACHÓV.   Wait a minute. Give me a minute. I have to catch my breath. Oh, my God! I'm a wreck! My head, my whole body ... I feel like a shish kebab. I can't stand it anymore. This is the end! Listen, don't ask questions, don't ask me for details — just be a real friend and give me a gun. Please!

MURÁSHKIN.   Now that's enough! You're acting like a crybaby! Listen to yourself! A man like you, a married man, with a good steady job ... You ought to be ashamed of yourself.

TOLKACHÓV.   A married man! That's the whole problem! You know what it means, being a married man? It means I suffer. It means I am a pack animal, a garbage collector. I am a slave, a serf; I am a coward who sits quietly waiting for the next disaster and hasn't got the brains to blow his brains out. I am a fool and an idiot. Why am I still alive? *(Jumps to his feet.)* Well? Tell me, why am I alive! Oh, what is the point of it all, this uninterrupted concatenation of mental and physical punishments? Hm? Look, I can understand sacrifice, I could suffer for ideas, or ideals, but to suffer for ladies' dresses and lightbulbs, no! A thousand times no! No, no, and no! This is the end! It's all over! I can't stand it anymore!

MURÁSHKIN.   Stop shouting! The neighbors will hear.

TOLKACHÓV.   Let the neighbors hear. I don't care! You won't give me a gun, someone else will, no problem, and then everything will be over and done with. At last. I've made up my mind, do you hear? I've made up my mind!

MURÁSHKIN.   Stop that! You've just ripped off one of my buttons! Get a hold of yourself, man! Now! Now, just what's so bad about your life? I don't understand any of this.

TOLKACHÓV.   What's so bad? You want to know what's so bad? All right, I'll tell you. I'll lay it all out for you in detail, in black and white, and then you'll know. And then maybe I'll feel better. Let's sit down, shall we? Good. Now. Just listen. *(Beat.)* My God. I'm always so short of breath. Now. Suppose we consider, just for example, today. Take today. All right? Now. As you know, I go to the office by nine and I stay until four, taking care of business. Now, it is hot in the office, and it is stuffy, and there are flies all over the place, and it is, as you very well know, a bottomless and never-to-be-enlightened outpost of chaos. My secretary is on vacation, my assistant, Krápov, has gone off somewhere to get married, and what is laughingly referred to as "the staff" is preoccupied with the joys of summer: weekends in the country, the possibility of illicit love affairs, and probably, for all I know, amateur theatricals. They're always asleep, or exhausted, or hungover, and you can't get a lick of work out of them. I have a temporary replacement of a secretary who is deaf in one ear — the left ear — and hopelessly in love. The clients haven't got a brain in their heads; you can't get them to sit still: They run, they jump, they get mad, they shout. The whole thing is beyond bedlam. It leaves you screaming for help. It is a disaster area, it is a nest of vipers, it is a zoo for incurables. And the work! Well, it's the same thing over and over again: Issue a certificate, write up a memo, issue a certificate, write up a memo. Monotonous. Like waves. Have you ever watched waves? Little ones? Very monotonous, waves. No variety. You know what I mean? Give me another drink of water ... So. Finally you leave the office. You are beaten into little bits. All you want is a drink and some dinner and a good night's sleep, but no! Because it dawns on you that it is summertime, and you have rented a place in the country for the summer, and that means you are an insignificant cog in the greater scheme of things, a niggling nothing, and now — do you follow me? — now you are about to flap around like a chicken with its head chopped off, because you have errands to run!

You see, we have a little custom out where we rent for the summer: If anybody is going into town, then any little sonofabitch whatsoever — and this is without even counting his own wife — has a perfectly natural, God-given right to give him a huge list of errands to run. My wife, for instance, wants me to go by the dress shop and tell them in no uncertain terms that the blouse is much too big ... except the shoulders, which are much too small. Sónya wants me to return her slippers, and my sister-in-law needs two-thirds of a yard of crimson silk to match this sample here and six yards of braid ... No, wait a minute — I can read you the whole thing. *(Takes a list from his pocket and reads.)* A globe for the lamp. One pound of smoked sausage. Cloves and cinnamon. Some castor oil for Mísha. Ten pounds of powdered sugar. Get the copper washtub and the sugar tongs from the house. Mothballs and bleach. Twenty bottles of beer. Smelling salts and a size eighty-two corset for Mademoiselle Chanceau. Oof! And bring out Mísha's galoshes and his fall jacket. *That* is my wife's list, and the family's. Now *here's* the list from all my dear friends and gentle neighbors, goddamn every one of them to hell. Tomorrow is Volódya Vlásin's birthday, so I'm supposed to buy him a bicycle. Colonel Víkhrin's wife is in what they call an interesting condition, so I have to go by the doctor's every other day and remind her to show up for the blessed event. And so on and so forth. I've got four different lists in my pocket and knots tied in my handkerchief for the rest of it. So there you are. Between the time you leave the office and the time your train leaves, you have to run all over town like a dog with its tongue in the mud, run run run run run, and curse the day you were born. The department store to the drugstore, the drugstore to the dress shop, the dress shop to the delicatessen, the delicatessen back to the drugstore. You're soaked in sweat, you keep dropping your money, the third stop you forget to pay and they carry on like you tried to rob them, the fourth stop a lady is wearing a long skirt and you step on it ... Oof! And what happens is, all this running around makes you crazy and turns you into a physical wreck, to the point where your bones crack all night long and you dream about crocodiles. So anyway, you finally get all your errands done, you've bought everything you're supposed to buy.

Now. Has it occurred to you that you may have a slight problem carting all this stuff out to the country with you? How, for example, do you pack a heavy copper washtub and a plunger and a lamp globe? And have you ever tried to make a single package out of twenty bottles of beer and a bicycle? You address the problem, you work at it like a Chinese puzzle, you try this way and that way, you wear out your ingenuity and your time trying to come up with something that will hold together, and of course something always falls out or rolls off at the last minute, no matter what you do, and when you get to the train station you have to stand there with your arms spread and your legs bowed, using your chin to hold on to a bundle held together with wire and tape and God knows what all. Finally the train arrives, and the crowd starts shoving and knocking your packages all over the place — you've got *your* things in *their* seats. They all start shouting, they get the conductor, they threaten to kick you off the train, and what can I do? I just stand there rolling my eyes, like a donkey with a stick in its mouth and a carrot up its ass.

So. Now comes the next round. I finally arrive at the cottage. And naturally what I'd like is what I'm entitled to: a couple of good stiff drinks and a little something to eat, and finally a little rest from the labors of the just. A little visit with Mr. Sandman! And I have a perfectly natural, God-given right to it, no? No!

That's *not* what happens. What happens is, my wife has been waiting for this moment all day long. So you barely get started on your soup, and all of a sudden — wham, bam, thank you very much — wouldn't it be lovely to go out this evening, the drama group is putting on a show, or there's a dance at the club ... And that's that. You can protest and protest, and it doesn't mean a thing. You are a married man, and the words "married man" in the summertime mean a dumb beast of burden; you can load him down with anything you want, and nobody even mentions animal rights. So you go, and start losing your eyesight watching *The Duke's Decadent Daughter* or something with a short French name, and you clap your hands whenever your wife pokes you, and you sit there fading faster and faster until you start hoping an early emphysema will carry you off. Or suppose you go to the dance at the club. Then you have to work fast and try to round up enough suckers for your wife to dance with, and if you can't find enough suckers, you wind up dancing with her yourself. Dancing dance after dance with her! You get home from the show or the dance and it's after midnight and you're no longer a human being, you're a piece of dead meat. But at least you have attained your goal, the summit of your day is at hand, you proceed to divest yourself of your garments, and you get into bed. Unbelievable luxury! You close your eyes, and you are about to sleep ... Everything is suddenly wonderful and comfortable; it is positively poetry. The children aren't crying or fussing in the next room, your wife is still out, your conscience is clear, you cannot imagine anything better anywhere ever. You begin to drift off ... you are falling asleep ... And suddenly — suddenly you hear a tiny noise! Mosquitoes! *(Leaps to his feet.)* Mosquitoes! Goddamn mosquitoes! Damn damn damn damn damn! Mosquitoes! *(Shakes his fist heavenward.)* The ninth plague of Egypt! They bzzz and bzzz, and it is such a sorry sound, such a sad, depressing sound, you almost feel sorry for them, but since *you* are the poor sonofabitch they are biting, you begin to itch. Then you scratch. For a whole hour you scratch. Then you light a cigarette and blow smoke at them and you swat at them and you put your head under the covers, and nothing works. Finally you say the hell with it and you just lie back and let them destroy you: Eat me, you monsters, eat me! Finally you begin getting used to the mosquitoes. And then suddenly the tenth plague of Egypt strikes! Your wife has come home; she is in the living room, and she has brought along her tenors, and they begin rehearsing show tunes for their next show. You see, they spend their days sleeping, these tenors, and their nights rehearsing show tunes. And tenors, by Christ, are a torment beside which mosquitoes are positively benign. *(Sings.)* "Never say thy youth was wasted ..." Or this: "Once more, love, before you, enchanted I stand ..." Oh, I tell you, tenors are mean and vicious. They attack the central nervous system, they pull your nerves shrieking from your body ... But I have discovered this little trick, you understand, and I use it against them, and it really seems to help. What I do is, I tap like this with my finger right here on my temple, right next to my ear. And I just go on tapping right here like this for the next four hours or so, until they all go away ... Water, please, water, I need a glass of water — I can't go on ...

Well, finally, there you are. It's morning, you haven't slept, and now you have to get up! And march on down to the station! And get on the train! And you run, because you're afraid you'll miss the train, and it is not a pleasant day; it is a miserable day! It's cold and rainy and you're freezing and the train is filthy! And then you get to town, and you go to the office, and the whole merry-go-round starts all over again. There. I've told you the whole thing, exactly as it happens. *That* is *life*. And that life, believe me, I can say in all seriousness, I would not wish on my worst enemy. It has made a wreck of me! I am ill, do you understand, physically ill! I suffer from shortness of breath. I have heartburn, my digestion is not functioning, my vision is blurred, and I am in constant fear of something ... You may not believe this, but I have become a psychopath. *(Glances quickly around him.)* You understand this is strictly between you and me. I'm even thinking of going to see one of those doctors, you know, a psych ... psychi ... Psychic! No, no, I mean a psychiatrist. I can feel myself coming down with something, friend, and it's not going to be very pretty. You see, in these moments of aggravation, of stupefaction, when the mosquitoes are biting and the tenors are singing, I suddenly get this blur in my eyes, and what happens is, I leap up and run all over the house, screaming, "Blood! Blood, Iago, blood!" And the funny thing is, I really do get the urge to stick a knife into somebody or break a chair over their heads. So ... you see what summertime can drive you to. And the worst of it is, nobody feels sorry for you, nobody knows how you feel, they all act as if it was perfectly normal. They even laugh. But I am a human being — you have to understand that — and *I want to live!* This isn't a comedy — it's a tragedy. Look, if you haven't got a gun you can lend me, at least tell me you know how I feel.

MURÁSHKIN.   Believe me, I know how you feel.

TOLKACHÓV.   I know. I can see that you know how I feel. *(Beat.)* Good-bye. I've got to pick up the sardines and the sausage, and then there's the toothpaste, and then I catch my train.

MURÁSHKIN.   Where exactly is it you're spending the summer?

TOLKACHÓV.   At Rotten River.

MURÁSHKIN.   *(Overjoyed.)* No! Rotten River! I don't believe it! Do you happen to know Ólga Fineberg? She's spending the summer there too!

TOLKACHÓV.   Do I know her? Of course I know her.

MURÁSHKIN.   Oh, I can hardly believe this! What a surprise! What a coincidence! Listen, this is really wonderful of you —

TOLKACHÓV.   What is?

MURÁSHKIN.   You've got to do me a little favor. You won't mind — I know you're a friend! You will, won't you? Promise me you will!

TOLKACHÓV.   Will what?

MURÁSHKIN.   Be a friend! Oh, promise me you will! First of all, say hello to Ólga and tell her you saw me and that everything's fine, just fine, give her my best, and second of all, just take this one little thing with you when you go: She asked me to buy her a sewing machine, which of course I did, but of course there was no way to get it out to her, but now you can take it with you! And also; there's this little cage with this little canary in it that has to go too, only you have to be very careful because the little door of the little cage is awfully loose and ... What's the matter? Why are you looking at me like that?

TOLKACHÓV.   A sewing machine ... A little cage with a little canary ... A little birdie ... a little yellow birdie ...

MURÁSHKIN.   Iván Ivánich, what's the matter with you? Why are you getting so red?

TOLKACHÓV.   *(Stamps his foot.)* Give me the goddamn machine! Give me the goddamn cage! Here! You want to ride me out there yourself? You want to play horsie? Go on, kick the horsie! Kill him! *(Makes two fists.)* Blood! Blood, Iago, blood!

MURÁSHKIN.   You're going crazy!

TOLKACHÓV.   *(Jumps him.)* Blood! Blood, Iago, blood!

MURÁSHKIN.   *(Horrified.)* He's gone crazy! *(Shouts.)* Help! Help! Somebody help! Help!

TOLKACHÓV.   *(Chases him around the room.)* Blood! Blood, Iago, blood!

CURTAIN.

SWAN SONG

A DRAMATIC SKETCH IN ONE ACT

1887

CHARACTERS

VASÍLY VASÍLICH SVETLOVÍDOV — an actor,
about 68 years old

NIKÍTA IVÁNICH — the prompter, an old man

The action takes place on the stage of a theater in the
provinces, late at night, after the show.

SWAN SONG

The empty stage of a second-rate provincial theater. Right, several crude unpainted doors leading to the dressing rooms; left and rear, piles of backstage junk. Center stage, an overturned stool. It's night. The stage is dark.

Enter from a dressing room Svetlovídov, costumed as Calchas from Offenbach's La Belle Hélène, *with a candle in his hand.*

SVETLOVÍDOV.   Well, if that isn't ... *(A loud laugh.)* What a joke! I fell asleep in the dressing room! The performance is over, everybody's gone home, and I slept through it all like a baby! Silly old fart. I must be getting old. Had a few too many, and I just sat there and went to sleep. Very smart. Brilliant performance. *(Shouts.)* Yégorka! Yégorka! Where are you, goddamn it? Petrúshka! They must've gone home ... God damn 'em. Yégorka! *(Picks up the stool, sits down on it, and sets the candle on the floor.)* There's nobody here. Just an echo. I gave each of them a big fat tip today, and now when I need them they're gone. Bastards probably locked up the theater, too. *(Shakes his head.)* Ohh, God! I'm still drunk. I drank too much at the benefit today, all that beer and wine. Jesus. I smell like a brewery. My mouth feels like it's got twenty tongues in it Ohh! I feel awful. *(Pause.)* ... really stupid. I've gotten to be an old drunk! I got shit-faced at the benefit, and I don't even know whose benefit it was. I feel like someone kicked me in the kidneys, my back is killing me, I've got the shakes ... cold all over, just like the grave. You don't give a damn about your health, do you? Asshole. You're too old for this anymore. *(Pause.)* You're old ... you can't pretend anymore. No getting away from it this time. Your life is over. Sixty-eight years down the drain, just like that. And it won't come back. The bottle's almost empty, just a little bit left in the

bottom. Dregs, that's what it is. That's just the way it is, Váska, my boy, that's just the way it is. Ready or not, it's time for your final role. The death scene. The undiscovered bourne. *(Stares straight ahead.)* I've been an actor for forty-five years, and this is the first time I've ever been onstage in the middle of the night. Yes. The first time. Curious. It's so dark out there ... *(Crosses down to the edge of the stage.)* Can't see a thing. Well, the prompter's box, a little, and the stage boxes, and the conductor's podium ... All the rest is darkness. A bottomless black hole, just like the grave, and death out there, waiting ... Brr! It's cold! There's a wind coming from somewhere ... You could scare up a ghost out of this darkness. God, I'm scaring myself. My skin's starting to crawl ... *(Shouts.)* Yégorka! Petrúshka! Where the fucking goddamn hell are you? *(Beat.)* I've got to stop using language like that, I've got to stop drinking, I'm an old man, I'm going to die ... Most people get to be sixty-eight, they start going to church again, they start getting ready ... ready to die. And you — look at you. God! Swearing, getting drunk ... Look at this stupid costume — how could I want people to see me like this? I better go change ... I'm scared ... If I stay here the rest of the night, I'll die. *(Starts to exit to the dressing room. Enter Nikíta Ivánıch from the dressing room door farthest U. He wears a long white dressing gown. Svetlovídov sees him, shrieks with horror, and staggers backward.)* Who's that? Who're you? What do you want? *(Stamps his feet.)* Who *is* that?
NIKÍTA IVÁNICH.   It's just me.
SVETLOVÍDOV.   Who're you?
NIKÍTA IVÁNICH.   *(Moving slowly toward him.)* Me. Nikíta Ivánich. The prompter. Vasíly Vasílich, it's me!
SVETLOVÍDOV.   *(Falls onto the stool, shaking and breathing heavily.)* Oh, my God ... Who? Is that you? Is that you, Nikíta? Wha ... what are you doing here?
NIKÍTA IVÁNICH.   I've been sleeping nights in one of the dressing rooms. Only, please, don't say anything to the manager ... I haven't got any other place to go.
SVETLOVÍDOV.   It's just you, Nikíta. Oh, my God, my God. I thought ... *(Beat.)* They had sixteen curtain calls tonight, and bouquets of flowers, and who knows what all, but nobody took the trouble to wake up an old man and help him home. I'm an old

man, Nikíta. I'm sixty-eight ... and I'm sick. I don't have any strength left. *(Grabs Nikíta's hand and starts to cry.)* Don't leave me, Nikíta! I'm old, I'm sick, I'm going to die ... I'm scared! I'm so scared!

NIKÍTA IVÁNICH. *(Gently, respectfully.)* Vasíly Vasílich, it's time for you to go home.

SVETLOVÍDOV. No, no, I can't! I haven't got a home! I can't! I can't!

NIKÍTA IVÁNICH. Oh, dear. Did you forget where you live?

SVETLOVÍDOV. I won't go back there — I can't! I'll be all alone, Nikíta. I haven't got anybody — no wife, no children, no family. I'm all alone; I'm like the wind in an empty field ... I'm going to die, and no one will remember me ... It's awful to be alone. No one to hug you, keep you warm, put you to bed when you're drunk ... Who do I belong to? Does anybody need me? Does anybody love me? Nobody loves me, Nikíta!

NIKÍTA IVÁNICH. *(Almost in tears.)* The audience loves you, Vasíly Vasílich!

SVETLOVÍDOV. The audience? Where are they? They've gone home to bed and forgotten all about me. No, nobody needs me, nobody loves me. No wife, no children ...

NIKÍTA IVÁNICH. Now, now, what are you getting all upset about...?

SVETLOVÍDOV. I'm a human being, aren't I? I'm still alive, aren't I? I've got blood in my veins, not water. And I come from a good family, Nikíta, a very good family. Before I got involved in show business I was in the army. I was an officer — I was an artillery officer. You should have seen me when I was young. I was so good-looking, I was clean-cut, strong, full of energy, full of life! Oh, my God, where did it all go? And what an actor I was, Nikíta, huh? *(Gets up, leaning on Nikíta's arm.)* Where did it go, all that? My God, I ... Tonight I looked out into that darkness, and it all came back to me, everything! That darkness swallowed up forty-five years of my life, Nikíta. But what a life! I look out into that darkness and I can see it all again, just like I see you now! My youth, my confidence, my talent, the women who loved me ... the women who loved me, Nikíta!

NIKÍTA IVÁNICH. Vasíly Vasílich, I think it's time for bed.

SVETLOVÍDOV.   When I was a young actor, and just beginning to feel how good I was, I remember, there was this one woman ... She loved me for my acting! She was tall, beautiful, elegant, young, innocent. She burned with a pure flame, like the dawn light in summer! One look from those blue eyes, that magic smile, you couldn't resist! I remember one time, I stood before her, just like I'm standing before you now. She was so beautiful that day, so beautiful, and she was looking at me — I'll never forget that look, not to my dying day. Her eyes like velvet, full of love, full of passion, the dazzle of her youth! I wanted her, I was mad for her, I fell to my knees in front of her ... *(His voice starts to trail off.)* And she said, you have to choose. Me or the theater. *(Beat.)* Give up the theater! You understand? She wanted me to give up the theater! She could make love to an actor, but marry one — never! And I remember that day; I was playing ... oh, it was some awful part, nothing but clichés, and I was out there onstage ... and all of a sudden my eyes were opened! And I realized then there was no holy art of acting, it was all lies and pretending, and I was just a toy, a slave to other people's pleasure, a clown! Just a cheap clown! That's when I realized what the audience was after, what they wanted from me! And after that I never believed the applause, the bouquets of flowers, the glowing reviews. It's true, Nikíta! They applaud me, they buy my photographs, but we are strangers to one another, and they think of me as trash, as a whore! They want to get to know me because I'm a celebrity — it flatters them — but they wouldn't lower themselves to let me marry one of their sisters or daughters! And I don't believe their applause! *(Falls back onto the stool.)* I just don't believe them anymore!

NIKÍTA IVÁNICH.   Vasíly Vasílich, you're scaring me ... You look just awful! Let's you and me go home. Come on now ...

SVETLOVÍDOV.   That's when I finally found out what it was all about, Nikíta. I understood what they were like, and that knowledge has cost me dear! After that — after that girl — I rushed off without any direction, didn't care what my life was like, never thought ahead. I played cheap parts, cynical parts, I played the joker, I seduced anyone I could get my hands on ... But what an actor I was, what an artist! And then I let my art go, I got vulgar and commercial, I lost the divine spark ... That black hole out there swallowed me up! I didn't realize it until now, but now, just now, when I woke up, I looked back, and I saw those sixty-eight years! I'm old! My life is over! I have sung my swan song! *(Sobs.)* I've sung my swan song!

NIKÍTA IVÁNICH.   Vasíly Vasílich! Don't be so upset. Just calm down, you poor man, just calm down ... Oh, my God! *(Shouts.)* Petrúshka! Yégorka!

SVETLOVÍDOV.   But what talent! What power! You can't imagine the power of my voice, of my emotions — how sexy I was, like a vibrating chord! *(Pounds his chest.)* In here! Right in here! I had it all! I'm all right — just let me get my breath ... Listen, Nikíta, just listen! *(Excited.)* This is from *King Lear*, you remember, on the heath, the storm, the rain, thunder and lightning ... Vroooom! Psssssssh! The heavens open, then comes:

> "Blow, winds, and crack your cheeks! Rage! Blow!
> You cataracts and hurricanoes, spout
> till you have drenched our steeples, drowned the cocks!
> You sulf'rous and thought-executing fires,
> vaunt-couriers of oak-cleaving thunderbolts,
> singe my white head! And thou, all-shaking thunder,
> strike flat the thick rotundity o' the world,
> crack Nature's molds, all germens spill at once
> that make ungrateful man!"

(Impatient.) Quick, the Fool! Give me the Fool's lines! I don't have much time!

NIKÍTA IVÁNICH.   *(Acts the Fool's part.)* "Oh, nuncle, court holy water in a dry house is better than this rain water out o' door. Good nuncle, in; ask thy daughters' blessing! Here's a night pities neither wise men nor fools!"

SVETLOVÍDOV.

> "Rumble thy bellyful! Spit, fire! Spout, rain!
> Nor rain, wind, thunder, fire are my daughters.
> I tax not you, you elements, with unkindness.
> I never gave you kingdom, called you children ... "

Not bad, huh? What power! What talent! What an artist! Another one now, something ... something from the old days! *(Gives a long, happy laugh.)* Something from *Hamlet!* I'll start. Where? Oh, I know ... *(Acts Hamlet.)* "Oh, the recorders! Let me see one. To withdraw with you — why do you go about to recover the wind of me...?"

NIKÍTA IVÁNICH.   "O my lord, if my duty be too bold, my love is too unmannerly."

SVETLOVÍDOV.   "I do not well understand that — will you play upon this pipe?"

NIKÍTA IVÁNICH.   "My lord, I cannot."

SVETLOVÍDOV.   "I pray you."

NIKÍTA IVÁNICH.   "Believe me, I cannot."

SVETLOVÍDOV.   "I do beseech you."

NIKÍTA IVÁNICH.   "I know no touch of it, my lord."

SVETLOVÍDOV.   "It is as easy as lying; govern these ventages with your finger and thumb, give it breath with your mouth, and it will discourse most eloquent music ..."

NIKÍTA IVÁNICH.   "... I have not the skill!"

SVETLOVÍDOV.   "Why, look you now, how unworthy a thing you make of me! You would play upon me, you would seem to know my stops ... and there is much music, excellent voice in this little organ, yet cannot you make it speak. 'Sblood, do you think I am easier to be played on than a pipe? Call me what instrument you will ... you cannot play upon me."

Bravo! Encore! Who says I'm old? I'm not old — that's all a fantasy! I can feel my strength coursing through my veins — it's my youth, my strength, my life! Nikíta, I'm not old — you can tell, can't you? Talent doesn't grow old! Wait a minute, I'm a little dizzy ... Oh, God ... am I going crazy? *(The sound of a door opening.)* What's that?

NIKÍTA IVÁNICH.   It must be Petrúshka and Yégorka coming back. Talent, Vasíly Vasílich! You have a great talent!

SVETLOVÍDOV.   *(Shouts, turning toward the sound.)* Here I am, my brave warriors! *(To Nikíta.)* Come on, let's go get dressed. I'm not old — that was all a fantasy, just a momentary weakness. *(Laughs joyfully.)* What are you crying for? You poor old man, what are you crying for? You mustn't do that. You really mustn't. *(Hugs him, with tears in his eyes.)* You mustn't cry. When you're an artist, when you've got talent, then you never get old, you're never alone, never sick — even death seems a petty thing ... *(Weeps.)* What am I talking about talent, Nikíta? No, we've sung our swan

38

song. I'm just a squeezed-out old lemon, a melting icicle, a rusty nail, and you ... you're just an old theater mouse. You're the prompter. Come on, let's go. *(They start off.)* Talent? No ... The only thing I ever played in Shakespeare was Fortinbras — and I'm getting a little old for that. Oh, yes. You remember that speech from *Othello*, Nikíta?

"... Oh, now forever,
farewell the tranquil mind! Farewell content!
Farewell the plumed troop and the big wars
that make ambition virtue! Oh, farewell,
farewell the neighing steed, and the shrill trump,
the spirit-stirring drum, the ear-piercing fife,
the royal banner and all quality,
pride, pomp and circumstance of glorious war!"

NIKÍTA IVÁNICH.   That's talent! You've got it! Real talent!

SVETLOVÍDOV.   And this one:

"Our revels now are ended ... We are such stuff
as dreams are made on, and our little life
is rounded with a sleep ... "

(His voice fades as he goes out with Nikíta.)

THE CURTAIN FALLS SLOWLY.

PROPERTY LIST

Candle (SVETLOVÍDOV)

SOUND EFFECTS

Door opening

THE PROPOSAL

A COMIC SKETCH IN ONE ACT

1888

CHARACTERS

STEPÁN STEPÁNICH CHUBUKÓV — a landowner
NATÁLIA STEPÁNOVNA (NATÁSHA) — his daughter
IVÁN VASSÍLIEVICH LÓMOV — their neighbor

The action takes place in Chubukóv's farmhouse.

THE PROPOSAL

A room in Chubukóv's farmhouse. Enter Lómov, wearing a tailcoat and white gloves. Chubukóv goes to meet him.

CHUBUKÓV.   By God, if it isn't my old friend Iván Vassílievich! Glad to see you, boy, glad to see you. *(Shakes his hand.)* This is certainly a surprise, and that's a fact. How are you doing?

LÓMOV.   Oh, thanks a lot. And how are you? Doing, I mean?

CHUBUKÓV.   We get by, my boy, we get by. Glad to know you think of us occasionally and all the rest of it. Have a seat, boy, be my guest, glad you're here, and that's a fact. Don't want to forget your old friends and neighbors, you know. But why so formal, boy? What's the occasion? You're all dressed up and everything — you on your way to a party, or what?

LÓMOV.   No, I only came to see you, Stepán Stepánich.

CHUBUKÓV.   But why the fancy clothes, boy? You look like you're still celebrating New Year's Eve!

LÓMOV.   Well, I'll tell you. *(Takes his arm.)* You see, Stepán Stepánich, I hope I'm not disturbing you, but I came to ask you a little favor. This isn't the first time I've, uh, had occasion, as they say, to ask you for help, and I want you to know that I really admire you when I do it ... Er, what I mean is ... Look, you have to excuse me, Stepán Stepánich, this is making me very nervous. I'll just take a little drink of water, if it's all right with you. *(Takes a drink of water.)*

CHUBUKÓV.   *(Aside.)* He wants me to lend him some money. I won't. *(To him.)* So! What exactly are you here for, hm? A big strong boy like you.

LÓMOV. You see, I really have the greatest respect for you, Stepán Respéctovich — excuse me, I mean Stepán Excúsemevich. What I mean is — I'm really nervous, as you can plainly see ... Well, what it all comes down to is this: You're the only person who can give me what I want and I know I don't deserve it of course that goes without saying and I haven't any real right to it either —

CHUBUKÓV. Now, my boy, you don't have to beat about the bush with me. Speak right up. What do you want?

LÓMOV. All right, I will. I will. Well, what I came for is, I came to ask for the hand of your daughter Natásha.

CHUBUKÓV. *(Overjoyed.)* Oh, mama! Iván Vassílievich, say it again! I don't think I caught that last part!

LÓMOV. I came to ask —

CHUBUKÓV. Lover boy! Buddy boy! I can't tell you how happy I am and everything. And that's a fact. And all the rest of it. *(Gives him a bear hug.)* I've always hoped this would happen. It's a long-time dream come true. *(Sheds a tear.)* I have always loved you, boy, just like you were my own son, and you know it. God bless you both and all the rest of it. This is a dream come true. But why am I standing here like a big dummy? Happiness has got my tongue, that's what's happened, happiness has got my tongue. Oh, from the bottom of my heart ... You wait right here, I'll go get Natásha and whatever.

LÓMOV. *(Intense concern.)* What do you think, Stepán Stepánich? Do you think she'll say yes?

CHUBUKÓV. Big, good-looking fellow like you — how could she help herself? Of course she'll say yes, and that's a fact. She's like a cat in heat. And all the rest of it. Don't go away, I'll be right back. *(Exit.)*

LÓMOV. It must be cold in here. I'm starting to shiver, just like I was going to take an exam. The main thing is, you have to make up your mind. You just keep thinking about it, you argue back and forth and talk a lot and wait for the ideal woman or for true love, you'll never get married. Brr ... it's cold in here. Natásha is a very good housekeeper, she's kind of good-looking, she's been to school ... What more do I need? I'm starting to get that hum in my ears again; it must be my nerves. *(Drinks some water.)* And I can't just *not* get married. First of all, I'm already thirty-five, and that's about what they call the turning point. Second of all, I have to

44

start leading a regular, normal life. There's something wrong with my heart — I've got a *murmur*, I'm always nervous as a tick, and the least little thing can drive me crazy. Like right now, for instance. My lips are starting to shudder, and this little whatsit keeps twitching in my right eyelid. But the worst thing about me is sleep. I mean, I don't. I go to bed, and as soon as I start falling asleep, all of a sudden something in my left side goes *drrrk!* and it pounds right up into my shoulder and my head ... I jump out of bed like crazy and walk around for a while and then I lie down again and as soon as I start falling asleep all of a sudden something in my left side goes *drrrk!* And that happens twenty times a night — *(Enter Natásha.)*

NATÁSHA.   Oh, it's you. It's just you, and Papa said go take a look in the other room, somebody wants to sell you something. Oh, well. How are you anyway?

LÓMOV.   How do you do, Natásha?

NATÁSHA.   You'll have to excuse me, I'm still in my apron. We were shelling peas. How come you haven't been by to see us for so long? Sit down ... *(They both sit.)* You feel like something to eat?

LÓMOV.   No, thanks. I ate already.

NATÁSHA.   You smoke? Go ahead if you want to; here's some matches. Beautiful day today, isn't it? And yesterday it was raining so hard the men in the hayfields couldn't do a thing. How many stacks you people got cut so far? You know what happened to me? I got so carried away I had them cut the whole meadow, and now I'm sorry I did — the hay's going to rot. Oh, my! Look at you! What've you got on those fancy clothes for? Well, if you aren't something! You going to a party, or what? You know, you're looking kind of cute these days ... Anyway, what are you all dressed up for?

LÓMOV.   *(A bit nervous.)* Well, you see, Natásha ... well, the fact is I decided to come ask you to ... to listen to what I have to say. Of course, you'll probably be sort of surprised and maybe get mad, but I ... *(Aside.)* It's awful cold in here.

NATÁSHA.   So ... so what did you come for, huh? *(Pause.)* Huh?

LÓMOV.   I'll try to make this brief. Now, Natásha, you know, we've known each other for a long time, ever since we were children, and I've had the pleasure of knowing your entire family. My poor dead aunt and her husband — and as you know, I inherited my land from them — they always had the greatest respect for your father and your poor dead mother. The Lómovs and the Chubukóvs have always been on very friendly terms, almost like we were related. And besides — well, you already know this — and besides, your land and mine are right next door to each other. Take my Meadowland, for instance. It lies right alongside of your birch grove.

NATÁSHA.   Excuse me. I don't mean to interrupt you, but I think you said "my Meadowland." Are you saying that Meadowland belongs to you?

LÓMOV.   Well, yes; as a matter of fact, I am.

NATÁSHA.   Well, I never! Meadowland belongs to us, not you!

LÓMOV.   No, Natásha. Meadowland is mine.

NATÁSHA.   Well, that's news to me. Since when is it yours?

LÓMOV.   What do you mean, since when? I'm talking about the little pasture they call Meadowland, the one that makes a wedge between your birch grove and Burnt Swamp.

NATÁSHA.   Yes, I know the one you mean. But it's ours.

LÓMOV.   Natásha, I think you're making a mistake. That field belongs to me.

NATÁSHA.   Iván Vassílievich, do you realize what you're saying? And just how long has it belonged to you?

LÓMOV.   What do you mean, how long? As far as I know, it's always been mine.

NATÁSHA.   Now wait just a minute. Excuse me, but —

LÓMOV.   It's all very clearly marked on the deeds, Natásha. Now, it's true there was some argument about it back a ways, but nowadays everybody knows it belongs to me. So there's no use arguing about it. You see, what happened was, my aunt's grandmother let your grandfather's tenants have that field free of charge for an indefinite time in exchange for their making bricks for her. So your grandfather's people used that land for free for about forty years and they started to think it was theirs, but then, when it turned out what the real situation was —

NATÁSHA.   My grandfather and my great-grandfather both always said that their land went as far as Burnt Swamp, which means Meadowland belongs to us. So what's the point of arguing about it? I think you're just being rude.

LÓMOV. I can show you the papers, Natália Stepánovna!

NATÁSHA. Oh, you're just teasing! You're trying to pull my leg! This is all a big joke, isn't it? We've owned that land for going on three hundred years, and all of a sudden you say it doesn't belong to us. Excuse me, Iván Vassílievich, excuse me, but I can't believe you said that. And believe me, I don't care one bit about that old meadow: It's only twelve acres, it's not worth three hundred rubles, even, but that's not the point. It's the injustice of it that hurts. And I don't care what anybody says — injustice is something I just can't put up with.

LÓMOV. But you didn't listen to what I was saying! Please! Your grandfather's tenants, as I was trying very politely to point out to you, made bricks for my aunt's grandmother. Now, my aunt's grandmother just wanted to make things easier and —

NATÁSHA. Grandmother, grandfather, father — what difference does it all make? The field belongs to us, and that's that.

LÓMOV. That field belongs to me!

NATÁSHA. That field belongs to us! You can go on about your grandmother until you're blue in the face, you can wear fifteen fancy coats — it still belongs to us! It's ours, ours, ours! I don't want anything that belongs to you, but I do want to keep what's my own, thank you very much!

LÓMOV. Natália Stepánovna, I don't care about that field either; I don't need that field; I'm talking about the principle of the thing. If you want the field, you can have it. I'll give it to you.

NATÁSHA. If there's any giving to be done, I'll do it! That field belongs to me! Iván Vassílievich, I have never gone through anything this crazy in all my life! Up till now I've always thought of you as a good neighbor, a real friend — last year we even lent you our threshing machine, which meant that we were threshing *our* wheat in November — and now all of a sudden you start treating us like Gypsies. *You*'ll give *me* my own field? Excuse me, but that is a pretty unneighborly thing to do. In fact, in my opinion, it's downright insulting!

LÓMOV. So in your opinion I'm some kind of claim jumper, you mean? Look, lady, I have never tried to take anybody else's land, and I'm not going to let anybody try to tell me I did, not even you. *(Runs to the table and takes a drink of water.)* Meadowland is mine!

NATÁSHA.   You lie! It s ours!

LÓMOV.   It's mine!

NATÁSHA.   You lie! I'll show you! I'll send my mowers out there today!

LÓMOV.   You'll what?

NATÁSHA.   I said I'll have my mowers out there today, and they'll hay that field flat!

LÓMOV.   You do, and I'll break their necks!

NATÁSHA.   You wouldn't dare!

LÓMOV.   *(Clutches his chest.)* Meadowland is mine! You understand? Mine!

NATÁSHA.   Please don't shout. You can scream and carry on all you want in your own house, but as long as you're in mine, try to behave like a gentleman.

LÓMOV.   I tell you, if I didn't have these murmurs, these awful pains, these veins throbbing in my temples, I wouldn't be talking like this. *(Shouts.)* Meadowland is mine!

NATÁSHA.   Ours!

LÓMOV.   Mine!

NATÁSHA.   Ours!

LÓMOV.   Mine! *(Enter Chubukóv.)*

CHUBUKÓV.   What's going on? What are you both yelling for?

NATÁSHA.   Papa, will you please explain to this gentleman just who owns Meadowland, him or us?

CHUBUKÓV.   Lover boy, Meadowland belongs to us.

LÓMOV.   I beg your pardon, Stepán Stepánich, how can it belong to you? Think what you're saying! My aunt's grandmother let your grandfather's people have that land to use free of charge, temporarily, and they used that land for forty years and started thinking it was theirs, but it turned out what the problem was —

CHUBUKÓV.   Allow me, sweetheart. You're forgetting that the reason those people didn't pay your granny and all the rest of it was because there was *already* a real problem about just who *did* own the meadow. And everything. But nowadays every dog in the village knows it belongs to us, and that's a fact. I don't think you've ever seen the survey map —

LÓMOV.   Look, I can prove to you that Meadowland belongs to me!

CHUBUKÓV.   No you can't, lover boy.

LÓMOV.   I can too!

CHUBUKÓV.   Oh, for crying out loud! What are you shouting for? You can't prove anything by shouting, and that's a fact! Look, I am not interested in taking any of your land, and neither am I interested in giving away any of my own. Why should I? And if it comes down to it, lover boy, if you want to make a case out of this, or anything like that, I'd just as soon give it to the peasants as give it to you. So there!

LÓMOV.   You're not making any sense. What gives you the right to give away someone else's land?

CHUBUKÓV.   I'll be the judge of whether I have the right or not! The fact is, boy, I am not used to being talked to in that tone of voice and all the rest of it. I am twice your age, boy, and I'll ask you to talk to me without getting so excited and whatever.

LÓMOV.   No! You think I'm just stupid, and you're making fun of me! You stand there and tell me my own land belongs to you, and then you expect me to be calm about it and talk as if nothing had happened! That's not the way good neighbors behave, Stepán Stepánich! You are not a neighbor, you are a *usurper*!

CHUBUKÓV.   I'm a *what*? What did you call me?

NATÁSHA.   Papa, you send our mowers out to Meadowland right this very minute!

CHUBUKÓV.   You, boy! What did you just call me?

NATÁSHA.   Meadowland belongs to us, and I'll never give it up — never, never, never!

LÓMOV.   We'll see about that! I'll take you to court, and then we'll see who it belongs to!

CHUBUKÓV.   To court! Well, you just go right ahead, boy, you take us to court! I dare you! Oh, now I get it, you were just waiting for a chance to take us to court and all the rest of it! And whatever! It's inbred, isn't it? Your whole family was like that — they couldn't wait to start suing. They were always in court! And that's a fact!

LÓMOV.   You leave my family out of this! The Lómovs were all decent, law-abiding citizens, every one of them, not like some

people I could name, who were arrested for embezzlement —
your uncle, for instance!

CHUBUKÓV.   Every single one of the Lómovs was crazy! All
of them!

NATÁSHA.   All of them! Every single one!

CHUBUKÓV.   Your uncle was a falling-down drunk, and that's a
fact! And your aunt, the youngest one, she used to run around
with an architect! An architect! And that's a fact!

LÓMOV.   And your mother was a hunchback! *(Clutches his chest.)*
Oh, my God, I've got a pain in my side ... my head's beginning to
pound! Oh, my God, give me some water!

CHUBUKÓV.   And your father was a gambler and a glutton!

NATÁSHA.   And your aunt was a tattletale; she was the worst
gossip in town!

LÓMOV.   My left leg is paralyzed ... And you're a sneak! Oh,
my heart! And everybody knows that during the elections, you
people ... I've got spots in front of my eyes ... Where's my hat?

NATÁSHA.   You're low! And lousy! And cheap!

CHUBUKÓV.   You are a lowdown two-faced snake in the grass,
and that's a fact! An absolute fact!

LÓMOV.   Here's my hat! My heart! How do I get out of here ...
where's the door? I think I'm dying ... I can't move my leg. *(Heads
for the door.)*

CHUBUKÓV.   *(Following him.)* And don't you ever set foot in this
house again.

NATÁSHA.   And you just take us to court! Go ahead, and see
what happens! *(Exit Lómov, staggering.)*

CHUBUKÓV.   *(Walks up and down in agitation.)* He can go to hell!

NATÁSHA.   What a creep! See if I ever trust a neighbor again
after this!

CHUBUKÓV.   Crook!

NATÁSHA.   Creep! He takes over somebody else's land and then
has the nerve to threaten them!

CHUBUKÓV.   And would you believe that wig-worm, that
chicken-brain, had the nerve to come here and propose? Hah?
He proposed!

NATÁSHA.   He proposed what?

CHUBUKÓV.   What? He came here to propose to you!

NATÁSHA.   To propose? To me? Why didn't you tell me that before!

CHUBUKÓV.   That's why he was all dressed up in that stupid coat! What a silly sausage!

NATÁSHA.   Me? He came to propose to me? Oh, my God, my God! *(Collapses into a chair and wails.)* Oh, make him come back! Make him come back! Oh, please, make him come back! *(She has hysterics.)*

CHUBUKÓV.   What's the matter? What's the matter with you? *(Smacks his head.)* Oh, my God, what have I done! I ought to shoot myself! I ought to be hanged! I ought to be tortured to death!

NATÁSHA.   I think I'm going to die! Make him come back!

CHUBUKÓV.   All right! Just stop screaming! Please! *(Runs out.)*

NATÁSHA.   *(Alone, wailing.)* What have we done? Oh, make him come back! Make him come back!

CHUBUKÓV.   *(Reenters.)* He's coming, he's coming back and everything, goddamn it! You talk to him yourself this time; I can't ... And that's a fact!

NATÁSHA.   *(Wailing.)* Make him come back!

CHUBUKÓV.   I just told you, he *is* coming back. Oh, God almighty, what an ungrateful assignment, being the father of a grown-up girl! I'll slit my throat, I swear I'll slit my throat! We yell at the man, we insult him, we chase him away ... and it's all your fault. It's your fault!

NATÁSHA.   No, it's your fault!

CHUBUKÓV.   All right, I'm sorry, it's my fault. Or whatever. *(Lómov appears in the doorway.)* This time you do the talking yourself! *(Exits.)*

LÓMOV.   *(Entering, exhausted.)* I'm having a heart murmur, it's awful, my leg is paralyzed ... my left side is going *drrrk!*

NATÁSHA.   You'll have to excuse us, Iván Vassílievich — we got a little bit carried away ... Anyway, I just remembered, Meadowland belongs to you after all.

LÓMOV.   There's something wrong with my heart — it's beating too loud ... Meadowland is mine? These little whatsits are twitching in both my eyelids ...

NATÁSHA.   It's yours — Meadowland is all yours. Here, sit down. *(They both sit.)* We made a mistake.

LÓMOV.   It was always just the principle of the thing. I don't care about the land, but I do care about the principle of the thing.

NATÁSHA.   I know, the principle of the thing ... Why don't we talk about something else?

LÓMOV.   And besides, I really can prove it. My aunt's grandmother let your grandfather's tenants have that field —

NATÁSHA.   That's enough! I think we should change the subject. *(Aside.)* I don't know where to start ... *(To Lómov.)* How's the hunting? Are you going hunting anytime soon?

LÓMOV.   Oh, yes, geese and grouse hunting, Natásha, geese and grouse. I was thinking of going after the harvest is in. Oh, by the way, did I tell you? The worst thing happened to me! You know my old hound Guesser? Well, he went lame on me.

NATÁSHA.   Oh, that's terrible! What happened?

LÓMOV.   I don't know; he must have dislocated his hip, or maybe he got into a fight with some other dogs and got bit. *(Sighs.)* And he was the best hound dog, not to mention how much he cost. I got him from Mirónov, and I paid a hundred and twenty-five for him.

NATÁSHA.   *(Beat.)* Ivan Vassílievich, you paid too much.

LÓMOV.   *(Beat.)* I thought I got him pretty cheap. He's a real good dog

NATÁSHA.   Papa paid only eighty-five for his hound dog Messer, and Messer is a lot better than your old Guesser!

LÓMOV.   Messer is better than Guesser? What do you mean? *(Laughs.)* Messer is better than Guesser!

NATÁSHA.   Of course he's better! I mean, he's not full grown yet, he's still a pup, but when it comes to a bark and a bite, nobody has a better dog.

LÓMOV.   Excuse me, Natásha, but I think you're forgetting something. He's got an underslung jaw, and a dog with an underslung jaw can never be a good retriever.

NATÁSHA.   An underslung jaw? That's the first I ever heard of it!

LÓMOV.   I'm telling you, his lower jaw is shorter than his upper.

NATÁSHA.   What did you do, measure it?

LÓMOV.   Of course I measured it! I grant you he's not so bad on point, but you tell him to go fetch, and he can barely —

NATÁSHA. In the first place, our Messer is a purebred from a very good line — he's the son of Pusher and Pisser, so that limp-foot mutt of yours couldn't touch him for breeding. Besides which, your dog is old and ratty and full of fleas —

LÓMOV. He may be old, but I wouldn't take five of your Messers for him. How can you even say that? Guesser is a real hound, and that Messer is a joke, he's not even worth worrying about. Every old fart in the county's got a dog just like your Messer — there's a mess of them everywhere you look! You paid twenty rubles, you paid too much!

NATÁSHA. Iván Vassílievich, for some reason you are being perverse on purpose. First you think Meadowland belongs to you, now you think Guesser is better than Messer. I don't think much of a man who doesn't say what he knows to be a fact. You know perfectly well that Messer is a hundred times better than that ... that dumb Guesser of yours. So why do you keep saying the opposite?

LÓMOV. You must think I'm either blind or stupid! Can't you understand that your Messer has an underslung jaw?

NATÁSHA. It's not true!

LÓMOV. He has an underslung jaw!

NATÁSHA. (Shouting.) It's not true!

LÓMOV. What are you shouting for?

NATÁSHA. What are you lying for? I can't stand any more of this. You ought to be getting ready to put your old Guesser out of his misery, and here you are comparing him to our Messer!

LÓMOV. You'll have to excuse me, I can't go on with this conversation. I'm having a heart murmur.

NATÁSHA. This just goes to prove what I've always known: The hunters who talk the most are the ones who know the least.

LÓMOV. Will you please do me a favor and just shut up ... My heart is starting to pound ... (Shouts.) Shut up!

NATÁSHA. I will not shut up until you admit that Messer is a hundred times better than Guesser!

LÓMOV. He's a hundred times worse! I hope he croaks, your Messer ... My head ... my eyes ... my shoulders ...

NATÁSHA. And your dumb old Guesser doesn't need to croak — he's dead already!

LÓMOV. Shut up! *(Starts to cry.)* I'm having a heart attack!

NATÁSHA. I will not shut up! *(Enter Chubukóv.)*

CHUBUKÓV. Now what's the matter?

NATÁSHA. Papa, will you please tell us frankly, on your honor, who's a better dog: Guesser or Messer?

LÓMOV. Stepán Stepánich, I just want to know one thing: Does your Messer have an underslung jaw or doesn't he? Yes or no?

CHUBUKÓV. Well? So what if he does? What difference does it make? Anyway, there isn't a better dog in the whole county, and that's a fact.

LÓMOV. But don't you think my Guesser is better? On your honor!

CHUBUKÓV. Now, loverboy, don't get all upset; just wait a minute. Please. Your Guesser has his good points and whatever. He's a thoroughbred, got a good stance, nice round hindquarters, all the rest of it. But that dog, if you really want to know, boy, has got two vital defects: He's old and he's got a short bite.

LÓMOV. You'll have to excuse me, I'm having another heart murmur. Let's just look at the facts, shall we? All I'd like you to do is just think back to that time at the field trials when my Guesser kept up with the count's dog Fresser. They were going ear to ear, and your Messer was a whole half mile behind.

CHUBUKÓV. He was behind because one of the count's men whopped him with his whip!

LÓMOV. That's not the point! All the other dogs were after the fox, and your Messer was chasing a sheep!

CHUBUKÓV. That's not true! Now listen, boy, I have a very quick temper, as you very well know, and that's a fact, so I think we should keep this discussion very short. He whopped him because none of the rest of you can stand watching other people's dogs perform! You're all rotten with envy! Even you, buddy boy, even you! The fact is, all somebody has to do is point out that some-body's dog is better than your Guesser, and right away you start in with this and that and all the rest of it. I happen to remember exactly what happened!

LÓMOV. And I remember too!

CHUBUKÓV. *(Mimics him.)* "And I remember too!" What do you remember?

LÓMOV. My heart murmur ... My leg is paralyzed ... I can't move ...

NATÁSHA. *(Mimics him.)* "My heart murmur!" What kind of hunter are you? You'd do better in the kitchen catching cockroaches instead of out hunting foxes! A heart murmur!

CHUBUKÓV. She's right — what kind of hunter are you? You and your heart murmur should stay home instead of galloping cross-country, and that's a fact. You say you like to hunt; all you really want to do is ride around arguing and interfering with other people's dogs and whatever. You are *not*, and that's a fact, a hunter.

LÓMOV. And what makes you think you're a hunter? The only reason you go hunting is so you can get in good with the count! My heart! You're a sneak!

CHUBUKÓV. I'm a what? A sneak! *(Shouts.)* Shut up!

LÓMOV. A sneak!

CHUBUKÓV. You young whippersnapper! You puppy!

LÓMOV. You rat! You rickety old rat!

CHUBUKÓV. You shut up, or I'll give you a tailful of buckshot! You snoop!

LÓMOV. Everybody knows your poor dead wife — oh, my heart! — used to beat you. My legs ... my head ... I see spots ... I'm going to faint, I'm going to faint!

CHUBUKÓV. And everybody knows your housekeeper has you tied to her apron strings!

LÓMOV. Wait wait wait ... here it comes! A heart attack! My shoulder just came undone — where's my shoulder? I'm going to die! *(Collapses into a chair.)* Get a doctor! *(Faints.)*

CHUBUKÓV. Whippersnapper! Milk sucker! Snoop! You make me sick! *(Drinks some water.)* Sick!

NATÁSHA. What kind of a hunter are you? You can't even ride a horse! *(To Chubukóv.)* Papa! What's the matter with him? Papa! Look at him, Papa! *(Screeching.)* Iván Vassílievich! He's dead!

CHUBUKÓV. I'm sick! I can't breathe ... give me some air!

NATÁSHA. He's dead! *(Shakes Lómov's shoulders.)* Iván Vassílievich! Iván Vassílievich! What have we done? He's dead! *(Collapses into the other chair.)* Get a doctor! Get a doctor! *(She has hysterics.)*

CHUBUKÓV. Oh, now what? What's the matter with you?

NATÁSHA. *(Wailing.)* He's dead! He's dead!

CHUBUKÓV. Who's dead? *(Looks at Lómov.)* Oh, my God, he *is* dead! Oh, my God! Get some water! Get a doctor! *(Puts glass to Lómov's mouth.)* Here, drink this ... He's not drinking it ... That means he's really dead ... and everything! Oh, what a mess! I'll kill myself! I'll kill myself! Why did I wait so long to kill myself? What am I waiting for right now? Give me a knife! Lend me a gun! *(Lómov stirs.)* I think he's going to live! Here, drink some water. That's the way.

LÓMOV. Spots ... everything is all spots ... it's all cloudy ... Where am I?

CHUBUKÓV. Just get married as soon as you can and then get out of here! She says yes! *(Joins Lómov's and Natásha's hands.)* She says yes and all the rest of it. I give you both my blessing and whatever. Only please just leave me in peace!

LÓMOV. Huh? Wha'? *(Starts to get up.)* Who?

CHUBUKÓV. She says yes! All right? Go ahead and kiss her ... And then get the hell out of here!

NATÁSHA. *(Moaning.)* He's alive ... Yes, yes, I say yes ...

CHUBUKÓV. Go ahead, give him a kiss.

LÓMOV. Huh? Who? *(Natásha kisses him.)* Oh, that's very nice ... Excuse me, but what's happening? Oh, yes, I remember now ... My heart ... those spots ... I'm so happy, Natásha! *(Kisses her hand.)* My leg is still paralyzed ...

NATÁSHA. I'm ... I'm very happy too.

CHUBUKÓV. And I'm getting a weight off my shoulders. Oof!

NATÁSHA. But all the same — you can admit it now, can't you? — Messer is better than Guesser.

LÓMOV. He's worse!

NATÁSHA. He's better!

CHUBUKÓV. And they lived happily ever after! Bring on the champagne!

LÓMOV. He's worse!

NATÁSHA. Better! Better! Better!

CHUBUKÓV. *(Tries to make himself heard.)* Champagne! Bring on the champagne!

CURTAIN.

PROPERTY LIST

Glass of water (LÓMOV)

THE DANGERS OF TOBACCO

A MONOLOGUE IN ONE ACT

1902

CHARACTERS

IVÁN IVÁNOVICH NYÚKHIN — the husband of a wife who runs a music and boarding school for young ladies

THE DANGERS
OF TOBACCO

The stage represents a lecture hall in a small-town social club. Nyúkhin makes an impressive entrance. He has long side-whiskers but no mustache and is dressed in an old, worn tailcoat. He crosses to the lectern, bows, and adjusts his vest.

NYÚKHIN. Ladies and — so to speak — gentlemen. *(Scratches his whiskers.)* Someone suggested to my wife that it might be nice if I gave some sort of lecture here today, open to the general public, with the proceeds to go to charity. That's fine with me. A lecture? Why not? Really, what do I care? Of course, you understand I am not a professor, I am devoid of academic degrees, but nonetheless, for almost thirty years now, and at considerable risk to my health and whatever, mind you, I have been working on problems of a scientific nature, pondering them, and occasionally I even write scholarly articles, if you can believe that ... what I mean is, not exactly scholarly but — if you'll excuse the expression — sort of scholarly. As a matter of fact, I have written a very interesting article entitled "The Problem with Insects." My daughters liked it a lot, especially the part about the bedbugs. I read it to them. Of course, then I tore it up. You can write about bedbugs all you want, you know, but the only thing that will get rid of them is boric acid. And we even had them in the piano.

As the subject of my lecture today I have chosen — I think I may put it that way — the harmful effects which can be observed in human beings as a direct result of indulgence in tobacco. I myself smoke, but my wife told me I should speak today about the dangers of tobacco, so of course there's nothing more to say, is there? Dangers? Why not? What do I care? You on the other hand, ladies

61

and gentlemen, will, I hope, devote your serious attention to what I am about to say, otherwise I really don't think we'll get anywhere. If there is anyone here who has qualms about a dry scientific lecture, anyone who doesn't like the idea, feel perfectly free not to listen, or leave if you want. *(Adjusts his vest.)* Let me make a special point of reminding any physicians who may be present that my lecture contains many useful observations for them, since tobacco, aside from its harmful effects, is also used in medicine. For instance, a fly placed in a container of tobacco will die, usually from nervous convulsions.

Tobacco is, so to speak, a plant ... Whenever I give a lecture, my right eye twitches a little. Sorry. Please don't pay any attention; it's just nerves. I am a very nervous man, generally speaking, and my eye began twitching in 1889, on September 13, actually that was the day my wife gave birth to Barbara — that's our fourth daughter. All my daughters were born on the thirteenth. Nonetheless *(Looks at his watch.)*, since our time is short, I think we had better stick to the subject of our lecture. I should point out, however, that my wife runs a music school and a private boarding school — that is, not exactly what you'd call a school but something ... sort of like a school. Now, just between you and me, my wife likes to complain about never having enough of anything, but the fact is she has managed to put, so to speak, a little something aside, maybe forty or fifty thousand. Of course, I don't have a penny to my name, not one ... But what's the point of talking about it? At the boarding school, I am in charge of the housekeeping department. I make all the purchases, take care of the help, do the accounts, manufacture the students' notebooks, keep the bedbugs under control, walk my wife's dog, catch the mice ... Last night one of my duties was to issue a premeasured amount of flour and butter to the cook, since the schedule called for pancakes for breakfast. Now, to make a long story short, today, when the pancakes were ready, my wife sent word down to the kitchen that three of our boarders would not be eating pancakes, since they had swollen glands. The result of this of course was that we had a few extra pancakes, and what exactly were we supposed to do with them? Well, at first my wife told us to put them in one of the storage closets, and then she thought it over; she thought it over and she said, "Oh, go ahead and eat them yourself, you old bag of bones." That's what she calls me when she's in a bad mood: bag of bones, or sometimes snake in the grass, or sometimes Satan. Now, I ask you, do I look like Satan? And she's always in a bad mood. Well, I didn't just eat those pancakes; I gobbled them down without even chewing, because I'm always very hungry. Yesterday, for instance, she wouldn't let me have any dinner. You're just an old bag of bones, she said; what's the use of feeding you?

However, *(Looks at his watch.)* we seem to be gossiping, and I think we've gotten a little off the topic. Let us continue. Although I'm sure you'd all rather be listening to some music — some show tunes or an aria ... *(Sings.)* "Our eyes shall never waver in the heat of the battle ..." I can't remember exactly what that's from ... Oh, by the way, I forgot to tell you that at my wife's music school I am not only in charge of the housework but I also teach all the courses in mathematics, physics, chemistry, geography, history, solfeggio, literature, and so on. We also offer dance, voice, and drawing lessons: My wife charges extra for them, although I am the dancing and voice instructor as well. Our school of music is located on Mutt Street, number thirteen Mutt Street. That's probably why my life is such a failure, living as I do at number thirteen. And all my daughters were born on the thirteenth, and our house has thirteen windows ...

Well, what's the point of talking about it? If you'd like to discuss any of this with my wife, you can stop by the school anytime; a school catalog is available from the man at the door for thirty cents a copy. *(Takes a few brochures from his pocket.)* Or you can get them from me if you'd like! Thirty cents a copy. Would anybody care for one? *(Pause.)* No? Twenty cents a copy? *(Pause.)* Too bad. That's right, number thirteen Mutt Street. I'm afraid I haven't been much of a success at anything; I've gotten old and stupid. And here I am, giving a lecture. I look perfectly happy up here, but what I'd really like to do is start screaming at the top of my lungs or run away someplace where nobody could ever find me. And there's nobody I can complain to; there are times when I even feel like crying ... You say, "Well, there's always your daughters ..." What daughters? I try to talk to them, they only laugh at me. My wife has seven daughters. No, excuse me, I think it's six ... *(Brightens.)* No, seven! Anna, the oldest, she's twenty-seven, and the youngest is seventeen.

Ladies and gentlemen! *(Looks around.)* I am not happy. I have grown into a half-wit, a non-wit, but essentially what you see before you is a very happy father. Essentially that's the way it's supposed to be, and I certainly wouldn't want anything different. If only you knew! I have lived with my wife for thirty-three years, and I can say that those were the best years of my life ... well, not exactly the best, you know, but ... so to speak. They have passed, to make a long story short, in one happy twinkling of an eye, and frankly I don't give a good goddamn anymore. *(Looks around.)* Anyway, I don't think she's here yet — yes, she is *not here* — so I can say whatever I feel like ... I'm really afraid. She terrifies me whenever she looks at me. And here's another thing: All my daughters are unmarried; they've been unmarried for a long time, which is probably because they're bashful but also because men never get the chance to meet them. My wife won't give parties, she never invites anyone to dinner, she's so cheap; she's a hateful, stuck-up old shrew, and that's why no one ever comes to see us, but ... now, this is confidential, just between you and me *(Goes to the edge of the platform.)* ... you can meet my wife's daughters on all major holidays at their aunt Natalie's — she's the one with rheumatism, who always wears a yellow dress with little black dots that makes her look as if she had cockroaches crawling all over her. She always serves something to eat, and if my wife's not around, you can also ... *(Gestures taking a drink.)* Of course, I have to point out to you that it only takes one little shot to get me drunk, which makes me feel good inside, but at the same time I get so sad I can't even tell you: I start thinking about when I was young, for some reason, and for some reason it makes me want to run away. If only you knew how it makes me want to run away! *(With intensity.)* Run away! Just dump everything and run and never look back. Where? I don't care where! Just run away from this cheap, vulgar, filthy life that has turned me into a pathetic old wreck, a pathetic old half-wit, run away from that stupid, petty, evil, evil miser of a woman I'm married to, run away from a wife who's tormented me for thirty-three years, from the music lessons and the kitchen and my wife having all the money, and from all the ugly, mean things I have to live with ... until I get to someplace far away, and then I'll stop in a field somewhere and stand there like a tree or a fence post, like a scarecrow, and stare up at the enormous sky, stand there all night just looking at the moon, the quiet, shining moon, and forget it all ... oh, if only I could forget it all! If only I could get out of this ugly old tailcoat I got married in thirty-three years ago, *(Tears off the coat and throws it to the floor.)* the one I give lectures in where the proceeds go to charity. Take that! *(Stomps on the coat.)* And that! I know, I'm old, I'm poor, I'm pathetic, just like this vest — the back is all worn and falling apart. *(Turns to show his back.)* But I don't need a thing! I'm better than all this, and I'm an honest man, I used to be young, I was smart, I went to the university, I had dreams, I wanted to be a decent human being ... Now I don't want anything! The only thing I need is peace and quiet ... just a little peace and quiet!

(Looks into the wings and quickly puts the coat back on.) However, my wife is now waiting in the wings. She's here. She's waiting for me. *(Looks at his watch.)* Well, I see my time is about up ... If she asks, would you mind saying that the lecture ... I'd be very grateful if you wouldn't mind saying that the old bag of bones — me, I mean — behaved ... with dignity. *(Looks toward the wings and coughs.)* She's watching. *(Raises his voice.)* As a consequence of which — the fact, I mean, that tobacco contains a powerful toxic agent, as I have just described — we see that smoking is by no means advisable, and I hope, so to speak, that my lecture here today on the dangers of tobacco will produce a beneficial effect. That's all I have to say. *Dixi et animam levavi. (Bows grandly and exits.)*

CURTAIN.

THE FESTIVITIES

A COMIC SKETCH IN ONE ACT

1891

CHARACTERS

ANDRÉY ANDRÉYEVICH SHIPÚCHIN — manager of a savings and loan branch office, a man in his forties; wears a monocle

TATYÁNA ALEXÉYEVNA — his wife, about twenty-five years old

KUZMÁ NIKOLÁYEVICH HEÉRIN — the office bookkeeper, an old man

NASTÁSYA FYÓDOROVNA MERCHÚTKINA — an old lady in a ratty overcoat

Bank depositors, tellers, etc.

The action takes place in the branch office of a savings and loan association.

THE FESTIVITIES

The manager's office. A door left leads into the bank. Two desks. The office is furnished with rather pretentious attempts at elegance: velvet chairs, a potted palm, statues, an Oriental rug, a telephone. It is noon. Heérin is alone; he wears felt bedroom slippers.

HEÉRIN. *(Yelling to someone beyond the door.)* Somebody run down to the drugstore and get me a bottle of aspirin, large size, and bring me a glass of water! How many times do I have to tell you? *(Crosses to his desk.)* I am one large ache from head to toe. I've been writing nonstop for the last four days and haven't had a wink of sleep. I sit here writing from morning to evening, and then I go home and write from evening to morning. *(Coughs.)* And I'm burning up! Chills, fever, cough, pains in my legs; and my eyes ... there's something wrong with my eyes. I must have conjunctions. *(Sits.)* Our stuck-up friend the manager, that useless sonofabitch, is giving a talk at the festivities today, a talk on "Our Bank: Present and Future." Mr. Show-off. *(Writes.)* Two ... one ... one ... six ... zero ... seven ... carry six ... zero ... one ... six ... He wants people to think he's such a big shot, but I'm the one who sits here and does all his work for him! He scribbles out a lot of highfalutin nonsense, but I'm the one who sits here day after day and checks his figures! Goddamn him to hell anyway. *(Scribbling his calculations.)* I've had about all I can take! *(Writes.)* That leaves one ... three ... seven ... two ... one ... zero ... He swore he'd reward me for my work. If the festivities come off without a hitch, and he manages to pull the wool over everybody's eyes, he swore I'd get a gold watch and a bonus of three hundred ... Well, we'll see ... *(Writes.)* And if I'm doing all this work for nothing, then brother, watch out! I'm a mean man. Get me mad enough, and I won't stop at

69

murder! I mean it! *(Offstage sound of voices and applause. Shipúchin's voice: "Thank you! Thank you! I'm really touched!" Enter Shipúchin. He wears a tailcoat and white tie. He carries a framed certificate they've just presented to him.)*

SHIPÚCHIN.   *(In the doorway, still talking to the group in the main room.)* My dear colleagues, believe me, I will treasure till the day I die this memento of our happy days together! Till the day I die, ladies and gentlemen! And thank you all once again! *(Blows them a few kisses, then crosses to Heérin.)* Kuzmá Nikoláyich! My dear, dear colleague! *(From time to time, as long as Shipúchin is onstage, assistants and tellers enter with forms for him to sign, then exit.)*

HEÉRIN.   Allow me to congratulate you, Andréy Andréyich, on this happy occasion, the fifteenth anniversary of our branch, and I hope and trust that —

SHIPÚCHIN.   *(Shakes his hand warmly.)* Thank you! Thank you so much! Well, this is a joyful day! *(Beat.)* Oh, what the hell! Give me a hug! That'll be our part of the festivities! *(A rather formal embrace.)* Delighted! Absolutely delighted! I don't know how to thank you for all your devoted service! If I, as manager of this bank, have been able to accomplish *anything* useful, it's only because I can always rely on the devotion of my colleagues! *(Sighs.)* Yes indeed, fifteen years! Fifteen years, or my name isn't Shipúchin! *(Brightly.)* Now! How is my speech coming along? Almost ready?

HEÉRIN.   Almost. I have about five pages to go.

SHIPÚCHIN.   Perfect. So I can have it by three this afternoon?

HEÉRIN.   As long as I'm not interrupted. There are only a few details left to work out.

SHIPÚCHIN.   Marvelous. Marvelous, or my name isn't Shipúchin! The festivities begin at four o'clock. But look, let me have the first half now, will you? That way I can rehearse a little. Let me see ... *(Takes the speech.)* I attach great importance to this speech. Enormous importance! This will be a sweeping statement of my professional credo, and I intend to dazzle them ... dazzle them, or my name isn't Shipúchin! *(Sits down and begins to read through the speech to himself.)* Oh, God, I'm tired! Had a migraine last night, couldn't sleep, this morning I had to run around to all these meetings, and then back here, all this excitement, the cheering. I'm all wound up ... tired ...

HEÉRIN.   *(Writes.)* Two ... zero ... zero ... three ... nine ... two... zero ... My mind's a blur of numbers ... Three ... one ... six ... four ... one ... five ... *(Scribbling his calculations.)*

SHIPÚCHIN.   Oh, by the way, there's one little thing. Your wife came by this morning; she says she wants to lodge a complaint against you again. Says last night you tried to attack her and her sister with a knife ... Now, really, Kuzmá Nikoláyich, what kind of behavior is that? Naughty naughty!

HEÉRIN.   Andréy Andréyich, let me ask you, as part of the festivities, to show a little respect for my considerable efforts here and keep your nose out of my family affairs. Please!

SHIPÚCHIN.   *(Sighs.)* Really, Kuzmá Nikoláyich, you are impossible! Look at yourself — well brought up, respectable ... but when it comes to women, you act like Jack the Ripper. Really! I don't understand why you dislike them so much ...

HEÉRIN.   And I don't understand why you like them so much! *(Pause.)*

SHIPÚCHIN.   The employees just gave me this beautiful certificate, and the directors, so I'm told, intend to present me with a desk calendar and some kind of trophy ... *(Fiddles with his monocle.)* Good, I say! Good, or my name isn't Shipúchin! These things aren't just petty trifles, you know. A bank's reputation requires a little pomp and circumstance! Of course ... well, you're like one of the family here, so I don't mind your knowing ... of course, I made up the certificate myself, and the silver trophy — I ordered that myself too ... And the gold frame for the certificate, that cost twenty-five rubles, but we couldn't do without it. Otherwise they'd accuse us of being cheap. *(Looks around.)* Look at this office! All this fine furniture! People call me petty, you know, because I want the front doorknobs polished, because I want all our tellers in brand-new ties, and a uniformed doorman at the entrance ... Not true! No, sir! These are not petty concerns! If a man wants to live like a pig at home, why not? Lie around drunk all weekend, why not? He can —

HEÉRIN.   Please, no invidious comparisons!

SHIPÚCHIN.   I'm not comparing anything! Really, you are impossible. As I was saying: If you want to lie around at home acting lower class, doing whatever you feel like, that's your privilege. But this is a bank! Things here have to be larger than life! Every little detail here must convey an overwhelming impression. We want our clients to be overawed! *(Picks up a scrap of paper from the floor and flicks it into the wastebasket.)* That is my great value to this bank: I augment its reputation. I improve the tone of the place — enormously! Enormously, or my name isn't Shipúchin! *(Glances at Heérin.)* Now look, my good friend, a delegation of the bank's directors will be arriving any moment now, and here you sit in your old bedroom slippers and that awful scarf ... And that ratty old jacket! What color do you call that? Couldn't you wear a tail-coat? Or at least a dress coat of some kind ...

HEÉRIN.   I'm more concerned with my health than with your directors. I've got a terrible fever and chills.

SHIPÚCHIN.   *(Upset.)* But you make such a sloppy impression! You're simply destroying the ambience I've tried to create here!

HEÉRIN.   When your delegation gets here, I'll go hide. Where's the problem? *(Writes.)* Seven ... one ... Seven ... two. . . one ... five ... zero ... I don't like sloppy impressions any more than you do ... Seven ... two ... nine ... *(Scribbling his calculations.)* I hate sloppy impressions! And I hope that you didn't decide to invite any of your women friends to the festivities today.

SHIPÚCHIN.   Why not? Don't be ridiculous ...

HEÉRIN.   I know you — you'll have the place full of them, just for the sake of your "ambience," but look: They'll spoil the entire event. With women, you've always got problems. Talk about sloppy impressions!

SHIPÚCHIN.   I beg to differ. The presence of women has an elevating effect on any social gathering!

HEÉRIN.   Sure ... For instance, your wife ... She seems like an educated woman, but last Monday she opened her mouth and put her foot right in it. It took me two days to get everything all smoothed over. Right in front of some clients, she asked me: "Is it true that my husband invested some of the bank's money in Dráshko-Práshko shares and then they went bankrupt? My husband is so worried about it!" Right in front of the clients! I don't know why you have to discuss bank business with her! One of these days her remarks will get you arrested!

SHIPÚCHIN. All right, all right, that's enough! You're depressing me! I'm trying to keep my mind on the festivities! Oh, but that reminds me ... *(Looks at his watch.)* My wife should be here shortly. I suppose I should have gone to the station to meet her, poor darling, but I had no time ... and I was so tired. Actually, I suppose, I'm not all that glad to see her. I mean, I'm glad, but I wish she could have spent another couple of days at her mother's. She'll want me to spend the whole evening listening to her talk about her mother, and the fact is, some of the directors had proposed a little ... bachelor outing this evening ... *(Giggles slightly, then groans.)* Oh, now look. I'm making myself nervous. When I'm all worked up like this, the least little thing makes me want to burst into tears! And I can't, not today! Today I must be joyful! Joyful, or my name isn't Shipúchin! *(Enter Tatyána Alexéyevna. She wears a chic raincoat and carries a small overnight bag on a shoulder strap.)*
SHIPÚCHIN. Oh, God. Speak of the devil.
TATYÁNA ALEXÉYEVNA. Darling! *(Runs to her husband; a prolonged kiss.)*
SHIPÚCHIN. We were just talking about you! *(Looks at his watch.)*
TATYÁNA ALEXÉYEVNA. *(Breathlessly.)* Did you miss me? Was everything all right without me? I haven't even been home yet — I came right here from the station. I have so much to tell you, you can't imagine. I simply can't wait! No, no, I won't stay, I just dropped by for a minute. *(To Heérin.)* Kuzmá Nikoláyich! Hello! *(To Shipúchin.)* Is everything all right at home? No problems?
SHIPÚCHIN. No problems whatsoever. And you've lost a little weight over the past week; you look wonderful ... Well, how was your visit?
TATYÁNA ALEXÉYEVNA. Couldn't have been better. Mama and Kátya send their love. And Vasíly said to give you a kiss from him. *(Kisses him.)* There! And Auntie sent you a jar of her homemade jam, and they're all mad at you for not writing. And Zína sends love and kisses too. *(Kisses him.)* And oh! Wait till you hear what happened! I'm still terrified, thinking about it! Wait till you hear! *(Beat.)* Darling, what's the matter? Aren't you glad to see me?

SHIPÚCHIN.   Oh, I am, I am, of course I am! Sweetheart! *(Kisses her. Heérin coughs with annoyance.)*
TATYÁNA ALEXÉYEVNA.   *(Sighs.)* Poor Kátya! Poor dear Kátya! I feel so sorry for her!
SHIPÚCHIN.   Now look, darling, we have our festivities all planned for this afternoon, the delegation from the directors' office will be here any minute now, and you're not really dressed ...
TATYÁNA ALEXÉYEVNA.   Oh, of course! The festivities! I forgot! Congratulations, to both of you! What a wonderful occasion ... That's right, the festivities ... I just adore celebrations. And what about that wonderful certificate you had framed for the people who work here? Will they present it to you today? *(Heérin coughs with annoyance.)*
SHIPÚCHIN.   *(Embarrassed.)* Darling, let's not talk about it now ... Really. You should go home and change.
TATYÁNA ALEXÉYEVNA.   I will, I will; give me a moment. I've just *got* to tell you what happened to me! The *whole* story! Well. You remember you took me to the station when I left, and got me settled on the train, and I found a seat next to that fat lady, and I started to read — you know how I hate casual conversations with strangers in trains. So I sat through three stops, never said a word to anyone, just kept reading. Well, eventually it grew dark, and I began having the most depressing thoughts! And there was this young man sitting across from me, not too bad-looking, dark curly hair ... Well, we started talking ... and then a sailor joined us, and some university student ... *(Laughs.)* And I was naughty — I told them I wasn't married! And the attention that got me! We laughed and chatted away until almost midnight. The dark-haired young man told the most amusing anecdotes, and the sailor sang song after song. I nearly died laughing! And then the sailor ... well, you know what sailors are like! When he found out my name was Tatyána, you know what he sang? He sang me that aria from *Eugene Onégin*, you know the one? Where he says he loves Tatyána? *(Sings, then bursts into gales of laughter.)* Isn't that the most charming thing you've ever heard? *(Heérin coughs with annoyance.)*
SHIPÚCHIN.   Now, Tánya, we're disturbing Kuzmá Nikoláyich. You go on home, darling. We can talk about this later ...
TATYÁNA ALEXÉYEVNA.   Oh, that's all right, that's all right,

let him listen; this is *completely* fascinating! I'm almost done. Anyway, Seryózha came to the station to meet me, and then this other young man turned up, a tax auditor, I think ... not bad-looking, but a little ... a little *limp*, if you know what I mean; you can always tell by the eyes. Anyway, it turns out he knew Seryózha, so Seryózha introduced me, and the three of us went off together ... It was a *perfect* evening ... *(From offstage: "No! Where do you think you're going? You can't go in there!" Enter Merchútkina.)*

MERCHÚTKINA. *(In the doorway, waving them off.)* Keep your hands to yourself! Is that any way to behave? I have to see your boss! *(Enters; to Shipúchin.)* Your Excellency, *sir!* My name is Merchútkina, Nastásya Fyódorovna Merchútkina. My husband works for the county health department.

SHIPÚCHIN. What can I do for you?

MERCHÚTKINA. Well, Your Excellency, here's what happened. My husband was out sick for five months, and while he was home in bed, trying to recover, he got fired! Without any kind of reason! And then when I went to pick up his back salary — you're not going to believe this — they deducted twenty-four rubles and thirty-six kopecks. "What for?" I said. "Well," they said, "he borrowed the money from the credit union, and repayment was guaranteed." What do you mean? I said. He'd never borrow money without telling me! Just let him even try! Your Excellency, I'm a poor woman with no one to protect me. All I get from people is insults; nobody wants to help me out.

SHIPÚCHIN. Let me see ... *(Takes her petition and stands there reading it.)*

TATYÁNA ALEXÉYEVNA. *(To Heérin.)* Oh, but I have to start at the beginning. All of a sudden last week I got this letter from Mama; she wrote that my sister Kátya was going out with this man who wants to marry her, his name is Grendelévsky. Very good-looking young man, quite charming, but no job and not a cent to his name. And the worst thing is, Kátya is crazy about him. Mama was at her wit's end; she wanted me to come right away and try to change Kátya's mind.

HEÉRIN. *(Severely.)* Please, you're interrupting my work! All this business about Mama and Kátya, I don't understand a word! And I have work to do.

TATYÁNA ALEXÉYEVNA.   Well, I like that! Can't you pay attention when a lady is speaking to you? Why are you in such a bad mood today? *(Laughs.)* You must be in love!

SHIPÚCHIN.   Excuse me, I really don't understand ... what is this all about?

TATYÁNA ALEXÉYEVNA.   Are you? Yes, you are! You're in love! You're blushing!

SHIPÚCHIN.   *(To Tatyána.)* Tánya darling, wait for me outside, will you? I won't be a moment.

TATYÁNA ALEXÉYEVNA.   Oh, all right. *(Goes out.)*

SHIPÚCHIN.   I don't understand any of this. I really think, madam, you've come to the wrong place. What you want has nothing to do with us. You'd better go see someone at the office where your husband worked.

MERCHÚTKINA.   Your Excellency, I've been going to see them for the last six months, and they wouldn't even read my petition. I was out of my mind with worry, but then thank God for my brother-in-law: He told me to come see you. "You go see Shipúchin," he said. "He's an influential man, he can take care of anything." So here I am. Please, Your Excellency, you've got to help me!

SHIPÚCHIN.   Mrs. Merchútkina, there is nothing we can do for you. Think: Your husband, so far as I can make out, worked for the health department, but this is a bank. We are a completely private commercial organization. Don't you understand that?

MERCHÚTKINA.   If you need proof that my husband was sick, I've got a doctor's certificate. Here ... See?

SHIPÚCHIN.   *(Irritably.)* Yes, I'm sure, I believe you, but I repeat, this has nothing to do with us! *(From offstage comes Tatyána's laugh, followed by much masculine laughter.)*

SHIPÚCHIN.   *(Glances at the door.)* She's keeping them all from working out there! *(To Merchútkina.)* This is quite out of the ordinary. A bit silly, really. Didn't your husband tell you where to go with the petition?

MERCHÚTKINA.   He doesn't know anything more than I do, Your Excellency. All he says is: "Get out of here! It's none of your business!"

SHIPÚCHIN.   Madam, let me say again: Your husband worked

76

in the county health department, but this is a bank! We are not an official entity! We are an independent commercial institution!

MERCHÚTKINA.   Yes, yes, yes, I know ... I understand, Your Excellency. So in that case, Your Excellency, couldn't you just have them pay me, say, fifteen rubles? I don't need it all at once.

SHIPÚCHIN.   *(Sighs with exasperation.)* Ohh!

HEÉRIN.   Andréy Andréyich, if this keeps on, I'll never be able to finish your speech!

SHIPÚCHIN.   I understand, I understand. *(To Merchútkina.)* This has really gone on long enough. Can't you understand that coming to us with this petition is ... well, it's like taking a petition for divorce to a drugstore! *(A knock at the door. Tatyána's voice off-stage: "Andréy! Can I come in?")*

SHIPÚCHIN.   *(Shouts.)* No, darling. Just give me a minute; I'll be right out! *(To Merchútkina.)* All right, they shortchanged you, but what am I supposed to do about it? Besides, madam, we are planning a few festivities here today, we're quite busy, and we're expecting some rather important people, so if you'll excuse me —

MERCHÚTKINA.   Have a heart, Your Excellency! I'm all alone in the world ... I'm just a poor, weak woman, and I'm worn out ... I just can't do it anymore, I just can't! The landlord is suing us, I have to take care of my husband and do the housework, and now my brother-in-law is out of a job too!

SHIPÚCHIN.   Mrs. Merchútkina, I really ... Look, I'm very sorry, but I have no time to talk to you! You're giving me a headache with all this ... And you are keeping us from our appointed tasks, and we don't have all that much time! *(Sighs; aside.)* What a mess, or my name isn't Shipúchin! *(To Heérin.)* Kuzmá Nikoláyich, could you please explain to Mrs. Merchútkina here ... Oh, I give up. *(Throws up his hands and goes out.)*

HEÉRIN.   *(Crosses to Merchútkina; severely.)* Yes? What can I do for you?

MERCHÚTKINA.   I'm just a poor, weak woman ... I know, you look at me and you think, "Oh, she's strong as an ox," but you just take a good look: There's not a bone in my body that doesn't hurt! I can barely stand, I've lost my appetite. I couldn't even taste my coffee this morning.

HEÉRIN.   I asked you, what can I do for you?

MERCHÚTKINA.   Please, tell them to give me fifteen rubles! I can wait till next month for the rest.

HEÉRIN.   But you've already been told quite clearly that this is a bank!

MERCHÚTKINA.   Yes, yes ... Do you need to see the doctor's certificate? I've got it right here ...

HEÉRIN.   Are you out of your mind, or what?

MERCHÚTKINA.   Look, dear, this is all perfectly legal, you know. I'm not asking for what doesn't belong to me.

HEÉRIN.   And I repeat: Are you out of your mind? Damn it, madam, I haven't got time to waste talking to you. I'm busy! *(Points to the door.)* Please! Just go!

MERCHÚTKINA.   *(Astonished.)* What about my money? When do I get it?

HEÉRIN.   You are not merely out of your mind — you have obviously lost whatever mind you had! *(Taps a finger against his forehead.)*

MERCHÚTKINA.   *(Offended.)* What do you mean? Well, I like that! Go knock on your own wife's head! My husband is a county official: You can't pull this kind of stuff on me!

HEÉRIN.   *(Furious; between clenched teeth.)* Get out of here!

MERCHÚTKINA.   Oh, no, no, no ... not on me!

HEÉRIN.   *(Between clenched teeth.)* If you don't get out of here this second, I'll call the doorman and have him throw you out! Out! *(Stamps his foot angrily.)*

MERCHÚTKINA.   Go on! You just try it! I'm not afraid of you! I've dealt with your kind before!

HEÉRIN.   I swear to God, I have never in my entire life met any-one so ... so *repellent*. Ohh! This is not helping my headache. *(Breathing heavily.)* Listen, you old eyesore! I will say this one more time. If you don't get out of here right now, I will tear you into little pieces personally! I am a mean man! I can make you a cripple for life! I won't stop at murder!

MERCHÚTKINA.   You just like to hear yourself bark! You don't scare me. I've dealt with your kind before!

HEÉRIN.   *(In despair.)* I can't take any more of this! She's making me sick! *(Crosses and sits at his desk.)* If he wants this bank full of women, then I'm not going to finish this speech! I can't!

MERCHÚTKINA.   All I want is what's legally mine! And look at you! Sitting around your office in bedroom slippers! Peasant! You ought to be ashamed of yourself! *(Enter Shipúchin and Tatyána Alexéyevna.)*

TATYÁNA ALEXÉYEVNA.   *(Following her husband.)* ... And the next night we went to the Berezhnítskys'. Kátya had on a light-blue silk with lace trimming, cut *very* low, and she wore her hair up, which suits her; I did it up myself. Oh, what a time we had! Dressing, doing our hair ... And of course we looked absolutely ravishing!

SHIPÚCHIN.   *(His migraine has started up again.)* Yes, I'm sure ... ravishing ... They'll be here any minute ...

MERCHÚTKINA.   Your Excellency!

SHIPÚCHIN.   *(At the end of his tether.)* Now what? What do you want?

MERCHÚTKINA.   Your Excellency! *(Points at Heérin.)* Do you know what he did, this ... this ... oh! He poked his forehead at me, like I was crazy ... You told him to help me, and instead he made fun of me, he said all these awful things! I'm just a poor, weak woman ...

SHIPÚCHIN.   Very well, madam, I will do what I can ... I'll see that something gets done ... later, not *now*! For *now*, will you please get out? *(Aside.)* My migraine's starting up again!

HEÉRIN.   *(Crosses to Shipúchin, quietly.)* Andréy Andréyich, call the doorman and have him throw her out on her ear! This can't go on!

SHIPÚCHIN.   *(Terrified.)* No, no! She'll raise a ruckus, and we'll have the whole neighborhood on our necks!

MERCHÚTKINA.   Your Excellency!

HEÉRIN.   *(Practically whining.)* I have to finish your speech! And I can't, not like this!

MERCHÚTKINA.   Your Excellency, when do I get my money? I need it right now!

SHIPÚCHIN.   *(Aside, outraged.)* What an *astonishingly* vulgar woman! *(To her, in a very controlled voice.)* Madam, I have already explained to you that this is a bank. We are a commercial institution. We are not connected with any government program whatsoever.

MERCHÚTKINA.   Please, Your Excellency, help me out! You're my only hope! Please! If the doctor's certificate isn't enough, I can get an affidavit from his office. Just tell them to give me my money!

SHIPÚCHIN.   *(At his wit's end.)* Ohh!

TATYÁNA ALEXÉYEVNA.   My *dear* madam, you have just been informed that you are interfering in the business of this bank. Really! Is this any way to behave?

MERCHÚTKINA.   Please, dear, help me out! There's no reason for them to get mad at me! I can barely eat anymore, and my coffee this morning had no taste whatsoever.

SHIPÚCHIN.   *(Worn out, to Merchútkina.)* How much did you say you needed?

MERCHÚTKINA.   Twenty-four rubles and thirty-six kopecks.

SHIPÚCHIN.   All right! *(Takes out his wallet, gives her money.)* Here's twenty-five rubles. Just take them and get out! *(Heérin coughs with annoyance.)*

MERCHÚTKINA.   Oh, thank you, Your Excellency, thank you! I'm so grateful! *(Tucks the money away in her dress.)*

TATYÁNA ALEXÉYEVNA.   *(Sits down on the edge of her husband's chair.)* Well, I suppose I should go home ... *(Looks at her watch.)* Only I didn't finish my story! It'll only take me a minute, and then I'll go! You'll never *believe* what happened! So anyway, we went to the Berezhnítskys'; it was an enjoyable evening, nothing special ... but of course Kátya's boyfriend Grendelévsky was there! Well, I had spent the day talking to Kátya, pleading with her, trying to get her to reconsider, and she did, and at the party that evening she broke off with Grendelévsky. Well, I thought, things couldn't have worked out better! I made Mama happy, I saved Kátya, and I thought: Good, now I can relax. And guess what happened? Just before dinner, Kátya and I went for a walk in the garden, and all of a sudden — *(bursts into tears.)* — and all of a sudden we heard a shot ... Oh, I can't be unemotional about this! *(Sniffles into her handkerchief.)* I really can't!

SHIPÚCHIN.   *(Hopelessly.)* Ohh!

TATYÁNA ALEXÉYEVNA.   *(Weeps.)* We ran to the gazebo, and there was poor Grendelévsky, lying there with a pistol in his hand ...

SHIPÚCHIN.   All right, that's enough! I can't stand it! I can't stand it! *(To Merchútkina.)* What do you want now?

MERCHÚTKINA.   Your Excellency, couldn't you get my husband his job back?

SHIPÚCHIN.   I can't stand any more of this! *(Weeps.)* I can't, I can't! *(Gestures with both hands to Heérin, despairingly.)* Get rid of her! For the love of God, get rid of her!

HEÉRIN.   *(Crosses to Tatyána Alexéyevna.)* You heard him! Out! Get out!

SHIPÚCHIN.   Not her, the other one — that ... that ... horrible old ... *(Points to Merchútkina.)* That one!

HEÉRIN.   *(Doesn't understand; to Tatyána Alexéyevna.)* Out! Out! *(Stamps his foot.)* Get out!

TATYÁNA ALEXÉYEVNA.   What? Me? Are you mad?

SHIPÚCHIN.   This is horrible! This is a disaster! Get her out of here! Get rid of her!

HEÉRIN.   *(To Tatyána.)* Out! Before I break your neck! I won't stop at murder!

TATYÁNA ALEXÉYEVNA.   *(Runs from him; he chases her.)* How dare you! You monster! Andréy! Help! Andréy! *(Circles the room.)*

SHIPÚCHIN.   *(Runs after them.)* Stop! Please! For God's sake, don't make so much noise! Think of my career!

HEÉRIN.   *(Chases Merchútkina.)* Get out of here! Somebody get her! Catch her! Cut her throat!

SHIPÚCHIN.   *(Screams.)* Stop! Please! Please! Stop!

MERCHÚTKINA.   *(Circles the room.)* Oh, my God! My God! My God!

TATYÁNA ALEXÉYEVNA.   *(Screams.)* Save me! Save me! Oh, this is awful! Just awful! *(Climbs onto a chair, then collapses onto the sofa, moaning and groaning.)*

HEÉRIN.   *(Chases Merchútkina.)* Catch her! Break her neck! Cut her throat!

MERCHÚTKINA.   Oh, my God, I'm going to faint! Ohh! *(Falls senseless into Shipúchin's arms. A knock at the door. A voice offstage announces: "The delegation from the board of directors!")*

SHIPÚCHIN.   Delegation ... reputation ... occupation ...

HEÉRIN.   *(Stamps his foot.)* Out! Out before I cut you up into little pieces! *(Rolls up his sleeves.)* Let me at her! I won't stop at murder!

(Enter the delegation: five men, all in tailcoats. One carries the desk calendar, another the silver trophy. Bank employees crowd in at the door behind them. Tatyána Alexéyevna is stretched out on the sofa, Merchútkina is in Shipúchin's arms. Both women whimper softly.)

A MEMBER OF THE DELEGATION. Dear Andréy Andréyich! As we cast a retrospective eye over the past of our financial institution and let our minds glide gratefully over the story of its constant growth and development, we are *most* gratified. True, in the early days, lack of available capital and a few frivolous investments, as well as a very confused idea of our corporate goals, led one inescapably to Hamlet's question, "To be or not to be," and of course there were always those who maintained we should shut the place down completely ... And then you came to take over our administration. Your knowledge, your energy, and your tact are the reasons for our extraordinary success and our remarkable expansion. The bank's reputation ... *(Takes in the scene; coughs nervously.)* The bank's reputation ...

MERCHÚTKINA. *(Moans.)* Oh! Ohh!

TATYÁNA ALEXÉYEVNA. *(Moans.)* Water! Water!

MEMBER OF THE DELEGATION. Er, reputation ... *(Coughs.)* You have raised the bank's reputation to a point where we now feel able to compete with even the most renowned foreign establishments ...

SHIPÚCHIN. *(Babbling.)* Delegation ... reputation ... occupation ... "Oh, never say thy youth has flown ..." "There was a little man, and he had a little house ..."

MEMBER OF THE DELEGATION. *(Going bravely on.)* So therefore, when we cast an objective glance at the present, we find ourselves eternally grateful to you, dear Andréy Andréyich *(His voice trails off.)* So therefore we would like ... we would like to ... *(The delegation goes out in confused embarrassment.)*

CURTAIN.

PROPERTY LIST

Gold-framed certificate (SHIPÚCHIN)
Forms (ASSISTANTS, TELLERS)
Petition (MERCHÚTKINA)
Desk calendar (DELEGATION)
Silver trophy (DELEGATION)

THE WEDDING RECEPTION

A PLAY IN ONE ACT

1889

CHARACTERS

YEVDÓKIM ZAHÁROVICH ZHIGÁLOV — a retired bureaucrat

NASTÁSYA TIMOFÉYEVNA — his wife

DÁSHENKA — their daughter

EPAMINÓNDAS MAXÍMOVICH APLÓMBOV — her fiancé

FYÓDOR YAKOVLYÓVICH REVÚNOV-KARAÚLOV — chief
petty officer, retired

ANDRÉY ANDRÉYEVICH NIÚNIN — an insurance salesman

ANNA MARTÍNOVNA ZMEYÚKHINA — a nurse's aide; wears a
dark-red dress

IVÁN MIKHÁILOVICH YATZ — a telegraph operator

HARLÁMPY SPIRODÓNOVICH DÍMBA — a Greek; owns
a bakery

DIMÍTRY STEPÁNOVICH MOZGOVÓY — a volunteer in the
coast guard

The Master of Ceremonies

Wedding guests, waiters, etc.

The action takes place in a reception room in
Andronov's restaurant.

THE WEDDING RECEPTION

A brightly lit hall. A long table set for a banquet. Waiters in tailcoats put finishing touches on the buffet. An offstage orchestra is playing the last section of a quadrille. Enter Zmeyúkhina, followed by Yatz, followed by the Master of Ceremonies.

ZMEYÚKHINA.   No! No! No!

YATZ.   *(Pursuing her.)* Yes! Yes! Yes! Please! Say yes!

ZMEYÚKHINA.   No! No! No!

MASTER OF CEREMONIES.   *(Pursuing them.)* Wait, wait, wait, you can't leave now — we're still dancing! What about the *grand rond? Grand rond, s'il vous plaît! (They exit. Enter Nastásya Timoféyevna and Aplómbov.)*

NASTÁSYA TIMOFÉYEVNA.   You ought to be in there dancing, instead of bothering me with all this talk.

APLÓMBOV.   I am *not* interested in twisting my feet into knots like that Spanish dancer — what's his name — Spinoza ... No, I am a serious person. I take no pleasure in silly entertainments. But we are not talking about dancing here. Excuse me, *Maman*, but I simply don't understand your behavior. For instance. In addition to a certain number of domestic articles, your daughter's dowry was to include two lottery tickets with winning numbers. Well? Where are they?

NASTÁSYA TIMOFÉYEVNA.   I have this splitting headache ... It happens every time the weather warms up like this ...

APLÓMBOV.   Don't try to change the subject. I just found out you pawned those tickets! Now excuse me, *Maman*, but that is petty larceny! And I am not speaking out of sheer egoisticism, I

87

don't need your tickets, but it's the principle of the thing. I refuse to let anyone put something over on me. I have been able to make your daughter happy, but unless I get those tickets, I swear she'll rue the day. I am a respectable man!

NASTÁSYA TIMOFÉYEVNA. *(Examining the table and counting places.)* One, two, three, four, five ...

WAITER. The cook wants to know what kind of sauce you want on the ice cream: rum, Madeira, or plain.

APLÓMBOV. Rum. And tell the manager there's not enough wine. Tell him to set out a few bottles of Haut-Sauternes. *(To Nastásya Timoféyevna.)* You also promised me you'd invite a general to the wedding luncheon. May I ask what's become of him?

NASTÁSYA TIMOFÉYEVNA. Now, dear, it's not my fault ...

APLÓMBOV. May I ask whose fault it is, then?

NASTÁSYA TIMOFÉYEVNA. Andréy Andréyich's. He came by yesterday and promised to bring a general to the reception, a real one. *(Sighs.)* He probably couldn't find one; otherwise he'd be here. I feel bad about it: She's our only daughter, and we've spared no expense, and we certainly hoped to have a general ... But I'm afraid —

APLÓMBOV. And another thing. Everybody — and you especially, *Maman* — knows that before I proposed to her, that telegraph person Yatz wanted to marry her. So why did you have to invite him today? You must have known what an insult that would be!

NASTÁSYA TIMOFÉYEVNA. Oh, please! Epaminóndas Maxímich, you've barely been married two hours, and you haven't stopped tormenting me and Dáshenka with all this talk. What are you going to be like a year from now? Really! You're getting to be a bore!

APLÓMBOV. Can't stand to hear the truth, can you? Fine! Never mind! But please, just try to act respectable. That's all I want out of my in-laws — respectability. *(Through the room come pairs of dancers, finishing the grand rond. The Master of Ceremonies is in the lead with Dáshenka. The final pair is Yatz and Zmeyúkhina, who stay behind as the rest of the dancers exit.)*

MASTER OF CEREMONIES. *(Shouts as he leads the dancers off.)* Promenade! Promenade, messieurs, dames, promenade! (Enter Zhigálov *and Dímba; they head for the buffet.)*

YATZ. *(To Zmeyúkhina)* Please! Please! You must!

ZMEYÚKHINA. Oh, you impetuous boy! I already told you, I'm not in voice today.

YATZ. Please! Please sing something! Just one note! Please! One single little note!

ZMEYÚKHINA. Oh, you! You'll wear me out! *(Sits and begins fanning herself.)*

YATZ. Don't be so cruel! Such a heartless creature, and such a glorious voice! A voice like that, excuse my expressivity, you shouldn't be in the medical profession, you should be on the concert stage. That final trill, that was divine! The one that went like this ... *(Sings.)* "I loved you once ..." Divine!

ZMEYÚKHINA. *(Sings.)* "I loved you once, but will love come again ..." Is that the one you mean?

YATZ. Yes! Yes! That's the one! Divine!

ZMEYÚKHINA. No, I'm afraid I'm not in good voice today. Here, fan me for a while, will you? It's so hot! *(To Aplómbov.)* Epaminóndas Maxímich, why are you looking so depressed? What's the matter? It's your wedding day! Smile!

APLÓMBOV. Marriage is nothing to smile about! You have to pay constant attention to the smallest details.

ZMEYÚKHINA. Oh, you're so unromantic, all of you! I can't breathe around you. I need a different atmosphere! Give me air! Give me another atmosphere! *(Sings a few phrases.)*

YATZ. Divine! Divine!

ZMEYÚKHINA. Fan me! Fan me, I feel faint! Faint! Why do I feel so hot?

YATZ. Because you're all sweaty —

ZMEYÚKHINA. What a vulgar thing to say! Really! How dare you use language like that!

YATZ. I'm sorry! I realize you're accustomed to high society, excuse the expression, but I'm just —

ZMEYÚKHINA. Oh, leave me alone! I need poetry, something uplifting. No, fan me, fan me, fan me ...

ZHIGÁLOV. *(To Dímba.)* How about another? *(Pours drinks.)* A man can drink around the clock if he wants to, you know. The only thing is, you can't neglect business. Never neglect business!

89

Well, special occasion, have a few drinks, why not? Here you go ... Bottoms up! *(They drink.)* Are there any tigers in Greece?

DÍMBA. Of course.

ZHIGÁLOV What about lions?

DÍMBA. Lions too. Of course. In Greece is everyting, in Russia is notting. In Greece is my father, my uncle, my brothers. Here in Russia is notting.

ZHIGÁLOV. Hmm ... What about whales? Do you have whales in Greece?

DÍMBA. Of course. Greece have everyting.

NASTÁSYA TIMOFÉYEVNA. *(To Zhigálov.)* Why are you drinking already? It's time to get everybody to the table. And don't pick at the lobster — that's for the general. If he ever gets here, I mean ...

ZHIGÁLOV. Lobsters! You have lobsters in Greece? I bet you don't have lobsters!

DÍMBA. Of course. In Greece everyting!

ZHIGÁLOV. Hmm ... What about assistant professors? You have those?

APLÓMBOV. I can just imagine the atmosphere you must have in Greece!

ZHIGÁLOV. A bunch of thieves too, probably. I mean, Greeks, right? They're like Gypsies or Armenians. They sell you a sponge, sell you a fish, and they're out to skin you alive. How about another?

NASTÁSYA TIMOFÉYEVNA. You've had enough! It's time we all sat down. It's already noon.

ZHIGÁLOV. Fine, let's get 'em to all sit down. *(Shouts.)* Ladies and gentlemen, lunch! Time to eat! Please, everybody! Come sit down!

NASTÁSYA TIMOFÉYEVNA. This way, everybody! Please! Luncheon is served!

ZMEYÚKHINA. *(Takes her place at the table.)* Poetry! I must have poetry! "But he, rebellious, seeks the storm, as if the storm could bring him peace!" Storms! I must have storms!

YATZ. *(Aside.)* What a woman! I'm in love! Head over heels in love! *(The orchestra plays a march. Enter Dáshenka, Mozgovóy, wearing his uniform, Master of Ceremonies, male and female Guests. Hubbub; they all take places at the table. A brief pause.)*

MOZGOVÓY.   *(Stands.)* Ladies and gentlemen! I have just one thing to say ... We have a lot of toasts and speeches to make today, so I propose we start right in. Ladies and gentlemen, here's to the happy couple! *(The orchestra plays a fanfare. Everybody shouts "Hurrah" and all clink glasses.)*

MOZGOVÓY.   Kiss the bride!

EVERYBODY.   Kiss the bride! Kiss the bride! *(Aplómbov and Dáshenka kiss.)*

YATZ.   Fabulous! Fantastic! Excuse my expressivity, ladies and gentlemen, but I have to give credit where credit is due: This is magnificent, just magnificent! This room, the table, the flowers ... everything first class! Just fabulous! But there's one thing missing to make it a triumph! Electric light, if you'll excuse the expression! Every country in the world has electricity except us!

ZHIGÁLOV.   *(Solemnly.)* Electricity. Hmm ... The way I see it, electricity is a scam. They give you a few wires and expect you to call it a miracle. No, gentlemen, you want light, you want something more than a few wires — you want something substantial, something a man can get ahold of. You want fire! Flames! Fire is nature's light; nothing artificial about it!

YATZ.   If you'd ever seen an electric battery, you'd change your mind.

ZHIGÁLOV.   I have no desire to see an electric battery. It's all a scam. Just a way to squeeze what they can out of people's pockets. We all know what they're up to ... As for you, young man, instead of sticking up for a scam, you'd do better to have a drink! And pour a couple for the rest of us! That's the way!

APLÓMBOV.   I couldn't agree more, Papa. Why all this talk about science? I have nothing against science, mind you, I can talk about science very scientifically if I have to, but this is not the time or place! *(To Dáshenka.)* Is it, *chérie?*

DÁSHENKA.   Some people are always trying to show off how educated they are and you can never understand what they're talking about!

NASTÁSYA TIMOFÉYEVNA.   I've never had any education,

thank God, and I've done very well, managed to marry off three daughters to decent husbands. *(To Yatz.)* And if you think we're all so uneducated, why did you come to the wedding? You should have stayed home with your educated friends!

YATZ.   Nastásya Timoféyevna, I have always had the greatest respect for you and your whole family, and about the electricity, believe me, I wasn't trying to show off. I merely wanted to propose a toast: I have always hoped for nothing more than a good husband for Dáshenka. And you know, Nastásya Timoféyevna, it's not easy to find a good man nowadays. Nowadays, most people marry for money —

APLÓMBOV.   That's an insulting thing to say!

YATZ.   *(Backs down.)* I didn't mean to insult anybody ... Of course I'm not referring to present company ... I was just ... I mean ... I'm sorry! Everybody knows you married her for love, the dowry means nothing to you, it's a mere trifle —

NASTÁSYA TIMOFÉYEVNA.   What do you mean, a trifle? You don't know what you're talking about! We gave him a thousand rubles cash, plus three fur coats and a complete set of furniture, all matching! Also a double bed! See if you can find a better deal on a dowry anywhere!

YATZ.   I didn't mean ... Furniture, of course, that's good, and the fur coats, but I was just ... I was just trying to explain that I didn't mean to insult anybody.

NASTÁSYA TIMOFÉYEVNA.   Well, don't! We're very fond of your family, and that's why we invited you to the wedding, and now you say all these awful things. And if you knew Epaminóndas Maxímich was marrying for money, why didn't you tell us sooner? *(Weepy.)* My poor little girl! And I nursed her, I raised her, I used to sing her to sleep, she's more precious to me than diamonds or rubies —

APLÓMBOV.   You mean you believe him? Thank you very much! *(To Yatz.)* And as for you, Mr. Yatz, you may be a friend, but I will not allow you to say such insulting things in what is practically somebody's *home.* I must ask you to leave immediately!

YATZ.   What did you say?

APLÓMBOV.   And I can only wish you would behave with a little more respectability — as I do, for example. I *said*, I am asking you to leave immediately! *(The orchestra plays a fanfare.)*
MALE GUESTS.   *(To Aplómbov.)* Stop this! That's enough! What's gotten into you? Sit down! Stop all this!
YATZ.   I didn't mean ... I mean ... I really don't understand. Of course, I'll leave if that's what you want. But before I go, I want those five rubles I lent you last year, so you could buy — excuse my expressivity — a plaid vest. All right. One more drink, and then I'll go. Only first I want my money!
MALE GUESTS.   That's enough! That's enough! Stop this! It's not worth making such a fuss!
MASTER OF CEREMONIES.   *(Shouts.)* To the parents of the bride! Yevdókim Zahárich and Nastásya Timoféyevna! *(Orchestra plays a fanfare. General hurrah.)*
ZHIGÁLOV.   *(Very emotional, bows to everyone.)* Thank you! Thank you all! I'm grateful to all our dear friends here for coming today and sharing this happy occasion with us. I'm overcome with emotion — and I don't want anyone accusing me of being cheap! You're all wonderful people, and everything I have is yours! Many, many thanks! *(Kisses Nastásya Timoféyevna.)*
DÁSHENKA.   Don't cry, Mama! I'm so happy!
APLÓMBOV.   *Maman* is overcome with emotion at the thought of parting from her darling daughter. But I advise her not to forget our recent conversation.
YATZ.   Don't cry, Nastásya Timoféyevna! Think: What are human tears? A petty psychological reaction, that's all.
ZHIGÁLOV.   What about mushrooms? They have mushrooms in Greece?
DÍMBA.   Of course. In Greece is everyting.
ZHIGÁLOV.   I mean those big white ones, you know? You probably don't have those ...
DÍMBA.   We have! Big white ones, yes. We have everyting!
MOZGOVÓY.   Harlámpy Spirodónich, it's your turn to make a speech! Ladies and gentlemen, let him make a speech!
EVERYBODY.   *(To Dímba.)* Speech! Speech! Your turn! Speech!
DÍMBA.   Spich? Spich? I'm not unnerstan ... What spich?

ZMEYÚKHINA.   No, no, you can't refuse! It's your turn! Go on, stand up! Speech!

DÍMBA.   *(Stands, embarrassed.)* What I can say ... Well, what's Russia and what's Greece? Okay, is Greek peoples in Greece and Russia peoples in Russia. Is also sailing across ocean *karavia* — how you say here? — boats. And on land is going railroads, all kinds ... We Greek peoples, you Russia peoples, that's all ... So, is my spich. Russia she's here, Greece she's over there. *(Enter Niúnin.)*

NIÚNIN.   *(Out of breath.)* Ladies and gentlemen, just a minute! Stop! Hold the feast! Nastásya Timoféyevna, excuse me — can I have a word with you? Over here. *(Takes Nastásya Timoféyevna into a corner.)* Listen ... The general's coming! I finally found one! God, I had to look everywhere, but I found a real one, very impressive. Of course, he's old, maybe eighty ... maybe even ninety ...

NASTÁSYA TIMOFÉYEVNA.   When will he get here?

NIÚNIN.   He's on his way now. You'll be delighted — wait till you see. A perfect general! A real hero! And not some old infantry officer or artillery; he's a naval officer! Actually, he's a chief petty officer, but that's the naval equivalent of a major general. The same thing. Better, even!

NASTÁSYA TIMOFÉYEVNA.   Now, Andréy, this isn't some kind of joke, is it?

NIÚNIN.   A joke? Me? Of course not! Stop worrying!

NASTÁSYA TIMOFÉYEVNA.   *(Sighs.)* It's just that I don't want to spend a lot of money for nothing ...

NIÚNIN.   Don't worry! He's a perfect general! Picture perfect! *(Raises his voice.)* Anyway, I said: "Your Excellency, you mustn't forget your old friends! Nastásya Timoféyevna," I said, "is very annoyed with you!" *(Crosses to the table and sits down.)* So then he says: "Excuse me, my boy, but how can I go to the wedding when I've never even met the bridegroom?" "Oh, Your Excellency," I said, "come on! Why be so formal? The groom," I said, "is a lovely young man, with a heart as big as all outdoors. And," I said, "this is not some half-pint pen pusher, Your Excellency; this man is a loan officer in a bank! Nowadays," I said, "even very respectable women work in banks." That convinced him! He slapped me on the back, offered me a Havana cigar, and said he'd be here. Please, ladies and gentlemen, don't start eating yet! Wait for the general!

APLÓMBOV.   But when is he coming?

NIÚNIN.   Right away! When I left him he was already putting on his galoshes. Please, wait, don't eat yet ...

APLÓMBOV.   Then we should have them play a march ...

NIÚNIN.   *(Shouts.)* Hey! You musicians! Give us a march! *(The orchestra plays a march. Pause. Enter a waiter.)*

WAITER.   *(Announcing.)* Mr. Revúnov-Karaúlov! *(Zhigálov, Nastásya Timoféyevna, and Niúnin rush toward the door. Enter Revúnov-Karaúlov.)*

NASTÁSYA TIMOFÉYEVNA.   *(Curtsies.)* Welcome, Your Excellency! *So* good of you to come!

REVÚNOV.   Well, yes! Lovely to be here!

ZHIGÁLOV.   We are simple people, Your Excellency, nobody rich or famous here, just plain folks, but don't think we're trying to do this on the cheap! No, believe you me, we've spared no expense! Welcome to our wedding!

REVÚNOV.   Yes, of course! Really lovely!

NIÚNIN.   Allow me to introduce everybody, Your Excellency! The newlyweds, Epaminóndas Maxímich Aplómbov and his brand-new wife! Iván Mikháilich Yatz, works at the telegraph office! And a foreigner of the Greek persuasion, a pillar of our local baking industry, Harlámpy Spirodónich Dímba. Ósip Lukích Babelmándevsky! And ... well, et cetera, et cetera; the rest are just small fry. Sit down, Your Excellency, please!

REVÚNOV.   Yes, yes, of course. Excuse me, ladies and gentlemen, but I need a moment alone with young Andréy here. *(Takes Niúnin aside.)* Look, I'm a little confused. Why do you keep calling me Your Excellency? I'm not a general! I'm only a chief petty officer: that's lower than a captain.

NIÚNIN.   *(Talks right into his ear, as if he were deaf.)* I know that, Fyódor Yakovlóvich, but just humor us! Let us call you Your Excellency, just for tonight! This family is ... well, patriarchal, let's say. They love titles and old-fashioned formality ...

REVÚNOV.   Well, I suppose, if that's the case ... All right. *(Goes to the table.)* Lovely. Really lovely.

95

NASTÁSYA TIMOFÉYEVNA. Please sit down, Your Excellency! It's an honor to have you here! Eat something, Your Excellency! You'll have to excuse us; I imagine you're used to fancy food. But we're just plain folks, I'm afraid ...

REVÚNOV. *(He's hard of hearing.)* What's that? Hmm ... Oh, yes. Lovely. *(Pause.)* Yes ... Time was, we were all just plain folks, and everybody was happy. Now, I ... I'm a man of simple tastes myself ... Young Andréy here stopped by today, asked me to come to your wedding. How can I go? I said. I don't even know them! I'd feel out of place ... And he said, Oh, no, they're very simple people, patriarchal, he said, just like the good old days, they'd be overjoyed to have you. Well, I said, then I suppose it's all right. Matter of fact, I'm delighted. It's a bore here at home by myself, so if going to the wedding will make these good people happy, fine, let's go!

ZHIGÁLOV. You really mean that, Your Excellency? I respect that. I'm a simple man myself, but not cheap, no, no, and I'm proud to meet a man with the same attitudes as me! Eat something, Your Excellency!

APLÓMBOV. How long have you been retired, Your Excellency?

REVÚNOV. Excuse me? Oh, yes, right, I forgot ... Yes ... Well, shouldn't we drink to the happy couple before we eat? Here's to them!

EVERYBODY. To the happy couple! Kiss the bride! Kiss the bride! *(Aplómbov and Dáshenka kiss.)*

REVÚNOV. Hee hee hee ... Yes, the happy couple! *(Pause.)* Yes ... Well, yes, time was, the good old days, we were all plain folks and we were all happy. Simple, but happy. I'm simple myself. Just love simplicity, in fact. I'm an old man now, retired thirty years ago ... I'm seventy-two ... yes. Of course, back then I had a fondness for the high life, but now ... *(Sees Mozgovóy.)* Yes ... Now, you, young man, you're a sailor. Am I right?

MOZGOVÓY. Yes, *sir!*

REVÚNOV. Aha! Well, yes ... The navy! Always the toughest outfit. Hard work on board ship, right? Have to keep your wits about you, keep your eyes and ears open. Every little word aboard ship takes on an enormous significance. For example: Tops'ls in the for'ard shrouds! Fors'ls! Mains'ls! Skip me up a scuttle in the scuppers! What does all that mean? Hee hee hee ... Sounds complicated, eh? But any ordinary sailor can tell you! Pretty clever, eh?

NIÚNIN. Here's a toast to His Excellency Fyódor Yakovlóvich Revúnov-Karaúlov! *(Orchestra plays a fanfare. Everybody shouts "Hurrah.")*

YATZ. Now, you were quite ... *expressive* just now, Your Excellency, about the hardships of the life on the bounding main. But do you think being a telegraph operator is easy? Nowadays, Your Excellency, everyone who works for the telegraph agency has to speak and write French and German! And the enormous skill it takes to send a message over the wires! Technical mastery, that's what you need! Here, listen, I'll show you. *(With his fork, he taps dots and dashes on the tabletop, imitating a telegraph operator at work.)*

REVÚNOV. But what does it say?

YATZ. It says: "Thank you, Your Excellency, for coming to our wedding reception." You think that was too easy? Listen to this one! *(Taps again.)*

REVÚNOV. Could you do that a little louder? I can't hear too well ...

YATZ. That one says, "Happy am I, madam, to be here in your arms at last."

REVÚNOV. Madam? Madam who? Well, yes ... *(Turns to Mozgovóy.)* For example, now, you're under way in a stiff breeze, what do you need? Tops'l! Fo'c'sle! Mizzen royal! Frame out the gunnels on the larboard! Got to know your orders: All hands to the for'ard spar, set your jib and jimbo! All hands on deck! And up they go to get the mizzen t'gallant aloft, and you get all hands on deck! Batten down the bit board! Out with your lugs'ls and stays'ls! Main topmast stays'l!

MASTER OF CEREMONIES. Ladies and gentlemen, if I may have your attention —

REVÚNOV. *(Goes right on.)* Yes indeed! And that's not all. Lots more! You have to know what they mean and shout 'em right. Up with the main brace bumpkin! Tighten the boom vang! It's easy when you know what that means. Haul on the sheets! You know what that means! Stays and braces! You know what that means!

NIÚNIN. *(To Revúnov.)* Fyódor Yakovlóvich, our hostess wishes you'd talk about something else. It's getting a bit boring.

REVÚNOV. Boring? Boring who? *(To Mozgovóy.)* All right now, young man! You're under way, under full sail, you're close-hauled on a starboard tack, and now you have to come about into the wind. So, you know what order to give? I'll tell you! All hands aloft, ready about, and haul as hard as you can! Hee hee hee ...

NIÚNIN. Fyódor Yakovlóvich, please! That's enough! Eat something!

REVÚNOV. And as soon as you get 'em all up there, then what do you do? I'll tell you! All hands look sharp, ready about! God, that's living, eh? You shout out your orders, the crew jumps to like lightning, and you watch the sails take the wind! What a moment! I tell you, it gets you! Nothing like a first-rate crew! I tell you, it gets you right here! *(Slaps his chest, turns away, and begins coughing.)*

MASTER OF CEREMONIES. *(Takes advantage of the pause.)* And now, to celebrate this happy, so to speak, occasion, let us all join as one and raise our glasses in a toast to our dear —

REVÚNOV. Well, yes! And you have to know them all! For instance, mizzen, mizzen royal, mizzen royal stays'l, mizzen t'gallant, mizzen t'gallant stays'l —

MASTER OF CEREMONIES. *(Annoyed.)* Can't somebody shut him up? We'll never get a chance to drink!

NASTÁSYA TIMOFÉYEVNA. We're simple people, Your Excellency, and I'm afraid we can't understand a word you're saying. Would you mind changing the subject? Please! Give us a break!

REVÚNOV. *(Can't hear a thing.)* Thanks just the same, I've already eaten. Cake? Did you say cake? Oh, thanks, thanks ... Yes, yes, good old cake, just like the good old days, I remember ... And that, young man, is happiness! Full sail, over the bounding main, not a care in the world, and then ... and then ... *(His voice begins to quiver.)* You have to come about into the wind! Yes, into the teeth of the wind! There's not a seafaring man on the ocean who doesn't feel his heart leap up at the thought of that maneuver! You hear a shout: "All hands aloft, ready about" — and a spark of electricity fires up the entire crew! From the captain on down to the cabin boy, everyone ready for anything ...

ZMEYÚKHINA.   Boring! Boring! *(Loud chorus of boos, groans, etc.)*

REVÚNOV.   *(Can't hear a thing.)* Thanks just the same, I've already eaten. *(Carried away by enthusiasm.)* What a moment! All hands standing by! All eyes on the officer in charge! Fores'l and mains'l braces on the right, tops'l yard on the left, mizzens, all waiting for the captain's commands! And then it all happens in an instant! Fores'l sheets away, jib sheets away, helm astarboard! *(Leaps to his feet.)* The ship turns into the wind, the sails began to flap, the commander shouts: "Braces, braces, look sharp!" And *he* looks sharp, doesn't take his eyes from the main tops'l, and finally he sees that sail begin to flap, and this is the tremendous moment now, and the command rolls like thunder from prow to stern: "Cast off main sheet, haul in the braces!" and everybody explodes into action. For a moment it's all bedlam, and then suddenly you're away again. The ship has come about! The maneuver is a complete success!

NASTÁSYA TIMOFÉYEVNA.   General, you're being rude! At your age! You ought to be ashamed!

REVÚNOV.   What? Oh, no, thank you, I've already eaten ...

NASTÁSYA TIMOFÉYEVNA.   I *said*, at your age you ought to be ashamed, General! You're being rude!

NIÚNIN.   *(Embarrassed.)* Look, ladies and gentlemen ... is this any time to make such a fuss? Really ...

REVÚNOV.   In the first place, I'm not a general. I'm a chief petty officer in the navy, and that's nowhere near a general ...

NASTÁSYA TIMOFÉYEVNA.   Well, if you're not a general, what did you take our money for? We didn't pay you to come here and be rude to everybody!

REVÚNOV.   *(Doesn't understand.)* What money?

NASTÁSYA TIMOFÉYEVNA.   You know what money! The money Andréy Andréyrich paid you! *(To Niúnin.)* And you should be ashamed of yourself too, Andréy! This is not the kind of officer I paid for!

NIÚNIN.   Please, please! Let's change this subject! It isn't worth making all this fuss —

REVÚNOV.   Paid for? Paid for? What does she mean?

APLÓMBOV.   Excuse me, but ... didn't you get twenty-five rubles from Andréy Andréyich here?

REVÚNOV.   What twenty-five rubles? *(Begins to understand.)* This is disgraceful! Now I understand! What a cheap trick!

APLÓMBOV.   Are you telling us you didn't get any money?

REVÚNOV.   Of course I didn't get any money! Somebody get me out of here! *(Goes up from the table.)* What a cheap, low-down trick! To make fun of an old man like this, a veteran member of the armed forces ... If any of you were respectable, I'd challenge you to a duel! But in this case ... *(Confused.)* Waiter! Where's the door? Get me out of here! Waiter! What a mean trick! What a low-down trick! *(Goes out.)*

NASTÁSYA TIMOFÉYEVNA.   *(Beat.)* Andréy, where's that twenty-five rubles?

NIÚNIN.   This is no time to talk about money! Where's your sense of occasion? Everybody's trying to have a good time, and you want to argue about God knows what ... *(Shouts.)* Here's to the bride and groom! Music! Let's have some music! Play us a march! *(The orchestra plays a march.)* Here's to the bride and groom!

ZMEYÚKHINA.   I am simply suffocating! Atmosphere! I must have a different atmosphere!

YATZ.   (Ecstatic.) Isn't she magnificent? Isn't she divine? *(General uproar.)*

MASTER OF CEREMONIES.   *(Trying to be heard.)* Ladies and gentlemen! On this so to speak happy occasion ...

CURTAIN.

PROPERTY LIST

Fan (ZMEYÚKHINA)
Drinks (ZHIGÁLOV)
Fork (YATZ)

SOUND EFFECTS

Orchestra march
Orchestra fanfare

NEW PLAYS

★ **THE PICTURE OF DORIAN GRAY by Roberto Aguirre-Sacasa, based on the novel by Oscar Wilde.** Preternaturally handsome Dorian Gray has his portrait painted by his college classmate Basil Hallwood. When their mutual friend Henry Wotton offers to include it in a show, Dorian makes a fateful wish—that his portrait should grow old instead of him—and strikes an unspeakable bargain with the devil. [5M, 2W] ISBN: 978-0-8222-2590-4

★ **THE LYONS by Nicky Silver.** As Ben Lyons lies dying, it becomes clear that he and his wife have been at war for many years, and his impending demise has brought no relief. When they're joined by their children all efforts at a sentimental goodbye to the dying patriarch are soon abandoned. "Hilariously frank, clear-sighted, compassionate and forgiving." –*NY Times.* "Mordant, dark and rich." –*Associated Press.* [3M, 3W] ISBN: 978-0-8222-2659-8

★ **STANDING ON CEREMONY by Mo Gaffney, Jordan Harrison, Moisés Kaufman, Neil LaBute, Wendy MacLeod, José Rivera, Paul Rudnick, and Doug Wright, conceived by Brian Shnipper.** Witty, warm and occasionally wacky, these plays are vows to the blessings of equality, the universal challenges of relationships and the often hilarious power of love. "CEREMONY puts a human face on a hot-button issue and delivers laughter and tears rather than propaganda." –*BackStage.* [3M, 3W] ISBN: 978-0-8222-2654-3

★ **ONE ARM by Moisés Kaufman, based on the short story and screenplay by Tennessee Williams.** Ollie joins the Navy and becomes the lightweight boxing champion of the Pacific Fleet. Soon after, he loses his arm in a car accident, and he turns to hustling to survive. "[A] fast, fierce, brutally beautiful stage adaptation." –*NY Magazine.* "A fascinatingly lurid, provocative and fatalistic piece of theater." –*Variety.* [7M, 1W] ISBN: 978-0-8222-2564-5

★ **AN ILIAD by Lisa Peterson and Denis O'Hare.** A modern-day retelling of Homer's classic. Poetry and humor, the ancient tale of the Trojan War and the modern world collide in this captivating theatrical experience. "Shocking, glorious, primal and deeply satisfying." –*Time Out NY.* "Explosive, altogether breathtaking." –*Chicago Sun-Times.* [1M] ISBN: 978-0-8222-2687-1

★ **THE COLUMNIST by David Auburn.** At the height of the Cold War, Joe Alsop is the nation's most influential journalist, beloved, feared and courted by the Washington world. But as the '60s dawn and America undergoes dizzying change, the intense political dramas Joe is embroiled in become deeply personal as well. "Intensely satisfying." –*Bloomberg News.* [5M, 2W] ISBN: 978-0-8222-2699-4

DRAMATISTS PLAY SERVICE, INC.
440 Park Avenue South, New York, NY 10016 212-683-8960 Fax 212-213-1539
postmaster@dramatists.com www.dramatists.com

NEW PLAYS

★ **BENGAL TIGER AT THE BAGHDAD ZOO by Rajiv Joseph.** The lives of two American Marines and an Iraqi translator are forever changed by an encounter with a quick-witted tiger who haunts the streets of war-torn Baghdad. "[A] boldly imagined, harrowing and surprisingly funny drama." *–NY Times.* "Tragic yet darkly comic and highly imaginative." *–CurtainUp.* [5M, 2W] ISBN: 978-0-8222-2565-2

★ **THE PITMEN PAINTERS by Lee Hall, inspired by a book by William Feaver.** Based on the triumphant true story, a group of British miners discover a new way to express themselves and unexpectedly become art-world sensations. "Excitingly ambiguous, in-the-moment theater." *–NY Times.* "Heartfelt, moving and deeply politicized." *–Chicago Tribune.* [5M, 2W] ISBN: 978-0-8222-2507-2

★ **RELATIVELY SPEAKING by Ethan Coen, Elaine May and Woody Allen.** In TALKING CURE, Ethan Coen uncovers the sort of insanity that can only come from family. Elaine May explores the hilarity of passing in GEORGE IS DEAD. In HONEYMOON MOTEL, Woody Allen invites you to the sort of wedding day you won't forget. "Firecracker funny." *–NY Times.* "A rollicking good time." *–New Yorker.* [8M, 7W] ISBN: 978-0-8222-2394-8

★ **SONS OF THE PROPHET by Stephen Karam.** If to live is to suffer, then Joseph Douaihy is more alive than most. With unexplained chronic pain and the fate of his reeling family on his shoulders, Joseph's health, sanity, and insurance premium are on the line. "Explosively funny." *–NY Times.* "At once deep, deft and beautifully made." *–New Yorker.* [5M, 3W] ISBN: 978-0-8222-2597-3

★ **THE MOUNTAINTOP by Katori Hall.** A gripping reimagination of events the night before the assassination of the civil rights leader Dr. Martin Luther King, Jr. "An ominous electricity crackles through the opening moments." *–NY Times.* "[A] thrilling, wild, provocative flight of magical realism." *–Associated Press.* "Crackles with theatricality and a humanity more moving than sainthood." *–NY Newsday.* [1M, 1W] ISBN: 978-0-8222-2603-1

★ **ALL NEW PEOPLE by Zach Braff.** Charlie is 35, heartbroken, and just wants some time away from the rest of the world. Long Beach Island seems to be the perfect escape until his solitude is interrupted by a motley parade of misfits who show up and change his plans. "Consistently and sometimes sensationally funny." *–NY Times.* "A morbidly funny play about the trendy new existential condition of being young, adorable, and miserable." *–Variety.* [2M, 2W] ISBN: 978-0-8222-2562-1

DRAMATISTS PLAY SERVICE, INC.
440 Park Avenue South, New York, NY 10016 212-683-8960 Fax 212-213-1539
postmaster@dramatists.com www.dramatists.com

NEW PLAYS

★ **CLYBOURNE PARK by Bruce Norris.** WINNER OF THE 2011 PULITZER PRIZE AND 2012 TONY AWARD. Act One takes place in 1959 as community leaders try to stop the sale of a home to a black family. Act Two is set in the same house in the present day as the now predominantly African-American neighborhood battles to hold its ground. "Vital, sharp-witted and ferociously smart." –*NY Times.* "A theatrical treasure…Indisputably, uproariously funny." –*Entertainment Weekly.* [4M, 3W] ISBN: 978-0-8222-2697-0

★ **WATER BY THE SPOONFUL by Quiara Alegría Hudes.** WINNER OF THE 2012 PULITZER PRIZE. A Puerto Rican veteran is surrounded by the North Philadelphia demons he tried to escape in the service. "This is a very funny, warm, and yes uplifting play." –*Hartford Courant.* "The play is a combination poem, prayer and app on how to cope in an age of uncertainty, speed and chaos." –*Variety.* [4M, 3W] ISBN: 978-0-8222-2716-8

★ **RED by John Logan.** WINNER OF THE 2010 TONY AWARD. Mark Rothko has just landed the biggest commission in the history of modern art. But when his young assistant, Ken, gains the confidence to challenge him, Rothko faces the agonizing possibility that his crowning achievement could also become his undoing. "Intense and exciting." –*NY Times.* "Smart, eloquent entertainment." –*New Yorker.* [2M] ISBN: 978-0-8222-2483-9

★ **VENUS IN FUR by David Ives.** Thomas, a beleaguered playwright/director, is desperate to find an actress to play Vanda, the female lead in his adaptation of the classic sadomasochistic tale *Venus in Fur.* "Ninety minutes of good, kinky fun." –*NY Times.* "A fast-paced journey into one man's entrapment by a clever, vengeful female." –*Associated Press.* [1M, 1W] ISBN: 978-0-8222-2603-1

★ **OTHER DESERT CITIES by Jon Robin Baitz.** Brooke returns home to Palm Springs after a six-year absence and announces that she is about to publish a memoir dredging up a pivotal and tragic event in the family's history—a wound they don't want reopened. "Leaves you feeling both moved and gratifyingly sated." –*NY Times.* "A genuine pleasure." –*NY Post.* [2M, 3W] ISBN: 978-0-8222-2605-5

★ **TRIBES by Nina Raine.** Billy was born deaf into a hearing family and adapts brilliantly to his family's unconventional ways, but it's not until he meets Sylvia, a young woman on the brink of deafness, that he finally understands what it means to be understood. "A smart, lively play." –*NY Times.* "[A] bright and boldly provocative drama." –*Associated Press.* [3M, 2W] ISBN: 978-0-8222-2751-9

DRAMATISTS PLAY SERVICE, INC.
440 Park Avenue South, New York, NY 10016 212-683-8960 Fax 212-213-1539
postmaster@dramatists.com www.dramatists.com